MW01515360

797,885 Books

are available to read at

Forgotten Books

www.ForgottenBooks.com

Forgotten Books' App
Available for mobile, tablet & eReader

Download on the
App Store

ANDROID APP ON
Google play

ISBN 978-1-330-31121-9
PIBN 10022857

This book is a reproduction of an important historical work. Forgotten Books uses state-of-the-art technology to digitally reconstruct the work, preserving the original format whilst repairing imperfections present in the aged copy. In rare cases, an imperfection in the original, such as a blemish or missing page, may be replicated in our edition. We do, however, repair the vast majority of imperfections successfully; any imperfections that remain are intentionally left to preserve the state of such historical works.

Forgotten Books is a registered trademark of FB &c Ltd.
Copyright © 2015 FB &c Ltd.
FB &c Ltd, Dalton House, 60 Windsor Avenue, London, SW19 2RR.
Company number 08720141. Registered in England and Wales.

For support please visit www.forgottenbooks.com

1 MONTH OF
FREE
READING

at

www.ForgottenBooks.com

———◆———

By purchasing this book you are
eligible for one month membership to
ForgottenBooks.com, giving you
unlimited access to our entire
collection of over 700,000 titles via
our web site and mobile apps.

To claim your free month visit:

www.forgottenbooks.com/free22857

* Offer is valid for 45 days from date of purchase. Terms and conditions apply.

Similar Books Are Available from
www.forgottenbooks.com

Beautiful Joe
An Autobiography, by Marshall Saunders

Theodore Roosevelt, an Autobiography
by Theodore Roosevelt

Napoleon
A Biographical Study, by Max Lenz

Up from Slavery
An Autobiography, by Booker T. Washington

Gotama Buddha
A Biography, Based on the Canonical Books of the Theravadin, by Kenneth J. Saunders

Plato's Biography of Socrates
by A. E. Taylor

Cicero
A Biography, by Torsten Petersson

Madam Guyon
An Autobiography, by Jeanne Marie Bouvier De La Motte Guyon

The Writings of Thomas Jefferson
by Thomas Jefferson

Thomas Skinner, M.D.
A Biographical Sketch, by John H. Clarke

Saint Thomas Aquinas of the Order of Preachers (1225-1274)
A Biographical Study of the Angelic Doctor, by Placid Conway

Recollections of the Rev. John Johnson and His Home
An Autobiography, by Susannah Johnson

Biographical Sketches in Cornwall, Vol. 1 of 3
by R. Polwhele

Autobiography of John Francis Hylan, Mayor of New York
by John Francis Hylan

The Autobiography of Benjamin Franklin
The Unmutilated and Correct Version, by Benjamin Franklin

James Mill
A Biography, by Alexander Bain

George Washington
An Historical Biography, by Horace E. Scudder

Florence Nightingale
A Biography, by Irene Cooper Willis

Marse Henry
An Autobiography, by Henry Watterson

Autobiography and Poems
by Charlotte E. Linden

THE AUTOBIOGRAPHY

OF

KARL von DITTERSDORF

The Autobiography

OF

KARL von DITTERSDORF

DICTATED TO HIS SON

Translated from the German

BY

A. D. COLERIDGE

LONDON

RICHARD BENTLEY AND SON

Publishers in Ordinary to Her Majesty the Queen

1896

[All rights reserved]

JUL 1 5 1940

196202

MUSIC LIBRARY

DEDICATED TO MY FRIEND

J. A. F. MAITLAND.

CONTENTS

CHAPTER X.

CHAPTER XI.

CHAPTER XII.

CHAPTER XIII.

CHAPTER XIV.

CONTENTS

CHAPTER XX.

CHAPTER XXI.

CHAPTER XXII.

CHAPTER XXIII.

CHAPTER XXIV.

CHAPTER XXV.

CHAPTER XXVI.

CHAPTER XXVII.

PREFACE.

THE autobiography of Karl Ditters von Dittersdorf, which was dictated from a sick-bed, and
finished only two days before the artist's death,
has a pathetic side, apart from the interest due
to the main story of his career. It was originally
published, with some few omissions and alterations, by Messrs. Breitkopf and Härtel, at the
beginning of this century, for the benefit of
Dittersdorf's widow. This act of kindness was
well bestowed.

It was a recognized fact that, as a *Volks-
componist*, the author of 'Der Apotheker' had
contributed in no small degree to the purity of
dramatic taste in Germany, occupying, in fact, a
position like that of Grétry in France—though

in depth of sentiment and literary distinction the Frenchman has far the best of it.

One single opera of Dittersdorf's still holds its own. Twelve of his instrumental compositions, however, were published as recently as 1866. By common consent he was, if not actually the first, among the first violinists of his day ; and higher gifts than those of a mere executant were needed to raise him to the level of an intimate friendship with two such pioneers of art as Gluck and Haydn. Bohemian as he was, Dittersdorf must have been an attractive personality. Gluck chose him for his travelling companion in Italy. Haydn and he together constituted themselves a jury of two, and used to retire regularly to consider their verdict on every novelty by the last composer whose works had been produced at Vienna. They found this process so wholesome to all concerned, that— Polonius fashion—Dittersdorf advises young, budding composers to practise it for their own advancement. The brilliant *virtuoso* became a power in music, and gained the esteem of no less a pundit than Padre Martini—perhaps the first theoretical musician of his time.

In his boyish days, when he was still a
member of the household of his kind patron,
the Prince of Hildburghausen, Vittoria Tesi,
the famous Italian *prima donna*, contributed
much to the formation of his taste. She was
well qualified to do so, for she had created
important parts in two of Handel's Italian
operas; and on the strength of her dramatic
successes in her native country, she had been
engaged at Vienna, in those days—according
to Burney — allowed by German critics to
be 'the Imperial seat of music as well as
of power.' Whether or no she set her cap at
the great composer, who shall say? He was
a confirmed bachelor—not over-polite to the
capricious people he had to deal with as *impresario*—and he made no attempt to secure her
for England. It has been said that perhaps he
objected to her practice of singing bass songs
transposed *all' ottava*, but this seems to me an
inadequate reason for rejecting her addresses.
It is something to her credit that she could
appreciate the genius of the young Saxon, and
be attracted by '*la lourde face emperruquée de
ce tonneau de porc et de bière qu'on nomme*

Haendel.'* Certain strange experiences of hers
are minutely recorded in the fourth chapter of
this volume ; they are in the main affirmed
by our own Dr. Burney, who found her still
living at the age of eighty, and one of the
celebrities of Vienna, in the year 1772. 'She
has been very sprightly in her day,' says he,
'and yet is at present in high favour with
the Empress Queen.' 'Sprightly' is a curious
epithet, and hardly, as we might expect, an
equivalent for 'no better than she should be '·
for unless an offer of marriage emanated from
herself, the 'sprightly one,' according to Dittersdorf, kept her many admirers at a distance.
Burney further informs us that she took up
with a man of great rank in Vienna, of near
her own age, 'probably,' adds the good Doctor,
'in a very chaste and innocent manner.' The
allusion is evidently to the Prince of Hildburghausen, who plays so large a part in this
memoir.†

* See the ' Letters of Berlioz.'
† Another of Tesi's friends, as she told Dittersdorf, was
Farinelli, the greatest of all singers in an age when many
were great. It was he who provoked the famous exclama-

If stage morality might have been improved in Dittersdorf's time, some leading ecclesiastics were not the men to head the crusade against laxity of life. I have heard of an Irish prelate who lived for fourteen years consecutively in Italy, and was allowed to administer the affairs of his diocese and console his clergy by far-off spirituality, without even the aid of a telephone; but such an ecclesiastic as the Prince-Bishop of Breslau, Dittersdorf's chief patron, is happily rare in our country. 'Shafgotsch,' says Carlyle, 'was a showy man of quality, nephew of the quondam Austrian Governor, whom Friedrich, across a good deal of Papal and other opposition, got pushed into the Catholic Primacy, and took some pains to make comfortable there, —Order of the Black Eagle, guest at Potsdam and the like;—having a kind of fancy for the airy Shafgotsch, as well as judging him suitable for this Silesian High-Priesthood, with his moderate ideas and quality ways—which I have

tion of the English lady: 'One God and one Farinelli!' It was he who charmed away the melancholy of *Philip V.* of Spain, and sang the same four songs to him, every night, for ten years!

heard were a little dissolute withal To the
whole of which Shafgotsch proved signally
traitorous and ingrate; and had plucked off
the Black Eagle (say the Books, nearly breath-
less over such a sacrilege) on some public
occasion, prior to Leuthen, and trampled it
under his feet, the unworthy fellow! Shafgotsch's pathetic letter to Friedrich, in the new
days posterior to Leuthen, and Friedrich's contemptuous, inexorable answer, we could give,
but do not; why should we?   O King, I know
your difficulties, and what epoch it is.   But, of
a truth, your airy dissolute Shafgotsch, as a
grateful "Archbishop and Grand - Vicar," is
almost uglier to me than as a traitor ungrateful
for it; and shall go to the devil in his own way!'

It is a mystery how such a man contrived to
retain his political influence ; but, owing to his
intervention at high quarters, Dittersdorf became
Knight of the Golden Spur, and he oddly rewarded his favourite Kapellmeister by turning
him into a sort of head-forester of Freienwaldau,
on which occasion, as the head-forester could not
possibly be anything but a noble, the author of the
'Apotheker' became 'Ditters von Dittersdorf.'

A strange world is depicted in this book. The modern baby appears to be, in some respects, less childish than the potentates who then controlled Europe. Life was a perpetual and rather a prosaic fairy-tale. Emperors were amused with islands that floated about of themselves, and bagpipe-players who capered and frisked like goats. Princes went out hunting, seated in an armchair, and took their pet sopranos with them. Sopranos—as will be seen—married theatrical wigmakers, in order to escape the importunities of Dukes. The senators of Venice did not disdain to punish a refractory artist, by making him sing before an executioner in disguise. As for Bishops, they seem to have occupied themselves principally in match-making, in the construction of operatic librettos, in the design of Turkish masquerades, and in hiding so many ducats in the snuffboxes or under the table-napkins of their favourite servants. Of anything serious, not a word! Dittersdorf was acquainted with the Emperor Francis and with Joseph II., Marie Antoinette's father and brother, and he did not die till the year 1799; but, apparently, he has never so much as heard of the French Revolution. Even the graver aspects of the art of music are, to a great extent, ignored; he mentions only 'the London Bach.'

The 'Autobiography,' which was a favourite book with Ferdinand Hiller, a man of letters as well as a composer, is valuable as the record of an artist's every-day life at the close of the last century. Dittersdorf, the honest chronicler of his own failures and successes, should have his say in England as well as in Germany. If not ornate, he is true. Haydn's imaginary talk, as given in George Sand's 'Consuelo,' is hard to reconcile with the language of Haydn's Diary. In this plain-spoken little volume we hear the very words uttered by men of genius, not those coined for them by others.

THE AUTOBIOGRAPHY OF
KARL von DITTERSDORF

CHAPTER I.

The first traces of my gift for music—I try my 'prentice hand in church.

I WAS born at Vienna on November 2, in the year 1739. My father, a native of Dantzig, held the office of *costumier* at Court and at the Theatre, in the days of Charles VI. He was a good draughtsman, too, and as such was chosen Lieutenant in command of the so-called Löbel - Bastey, a fortress armed with twenty cannon, during the Bavarian War, which broke out after the death of Charles VI., when Charles VII. was Emperor of Bavaria.

His success in life enabled him to give a somewhat better education to his five children than ordinary civilians can afford. I was the second of his three sons. We were sent to a Jesuit school, and, besides that, we were taught by a secular priest, who was boarded and lodged at my father's cost. I owe to this good man, who was neither a fanatic nor a freethinker, whatever religious principles and liberality of mind I can boast of. My father spoke French fluently, and all five of us had lessons in that language. He had musical tastes, too, and gave my eldest brother lessons on the violin.

I was barely seven years old when I discovered my own strong inclination for music, and entreated my father to give me lessons also. My request was granted, and I made such progress in the course of two years and a half, that my teacher (König was the good man's name) owned to my father that he had taught me all he knew, and that I must have another master to bring me up to concert pitch. 'It is a point of conscience with me,' said he, 'to give up your boy Karl, for he is a clever fellow, and certain to play far better than I can.' Would that all the world were as honest as König! My father, touched by the nobility of his conduct, made him a handsome present, and guaranteed him against loss of income by taking him on as teacher for my third brother.

My second violin-master was Joseph Zügler,* who was not only a first-rate player, but a good composer of chamber music. He took infinite pains with me, as an industrious and eager pupil. Being anxious to improve my reading at sight, he advised my regular attendance, every Sunday and Saint's Day, at the Roman Catholic Church, giving preference to the choir of the Benedictines at the Asylum, where there was a well-appointed orchestra, and the best masses, motets, vespers and litanies were sung.

I went the very next Sunday, and called upon the precentor, Gsur, that I might ask his permission to join the band. After staring at me from top to toe, he growled out ·

'Oh, I dare say! You are mistaken, if you think there's a place here for every young fiddle-scraper.

I was young, to be sure, but *fiddle-scraper* put my back up, and I rounded on him at once ·

How can you know whether I am fit to play or not? If I were not, do you suppose Mr. Joseph Zügler, my master, would have advised me to come to you as a candidate?'

* The man's real name was Ziegler. See 'The Dictionary of Music,' article 'Dittersdorf.'

He softened at this, and became quite pleasant.

'If Zügler really sent you, all right; I shall be very glad.'

Whereupon he told them to give me a violin, and showed me my seat next to the leader of the orchestra, Karl Huber, who watched me like a cat, to see if I played correctly, and actually stopped himself when the fugue began, in order to observe whether my rests were right. I did not miss a note.

'Bravo, my son!' said he, when it was all over. 'I could not have believed it.'

Gsur, who had also been on the look-out, expressed his pleasure at my performance, kindly assuring me that I might come whenever I pleased, the oftener the better.

'That's a very different thing!' thought I.

No wonder if I went home several inches taller than I came.

Thus it happened that, wherever Church music was going on, there was I taking a part, and this continued for a whole year. Nothing came amiss to me when I was in the band; I had such constant practice that I became a good orchestral player—quite a *devourer of notes*, as they say.

In the course of that year, it chanced that

Huber often had to play solos in church. His bowing, his method, his intonation, the whole performance, greatly impressed me. I spared no pains to imitate him, and on one occasion, when we were playing a Mass, containing a violin solo which I had never seen before, Huber said :

' Have you the courage to attempt it ?'

' I will have a try at it,' said I, ' though I cannot pretend to play it as well as you would.'

' Oh, fire away !' said he. ' You will do it right enough.'

And he handed me his own violin.

I did play the solo, though my heart was in my mouth to start with. I was consoled by feeling that the music went so unusually well that all my nervousness vanished, and when the first passages and modulations were repeated in the last movement, I varied them quite in the Huber style, so that all who heard me applauded.

I allude to this fact in all modesty, having no wish to boast of my talent as a youngster ; but I could not pass over the story, for it occasionally happens that more trifling matters than this may turn the current of men's lives ; and the incident had a marked influence on the whole of my subsequent career.

CHAPTER II.

My first introduction to the *Prince* of Hildburghausen, and the reception he gave me—Kapellmeister Bonno.

IT was customary for connoisseurs of music to attend the Benedictine Church in large numbers, for the music, particularly on great festivals, was of the choicest kind, and the performance first-rate. Some of Huber's admirers were sitting below when I played, and after the solo had finished they were loud in their praises, in the belief that they had been listening to Huber himself. But what was their surprise when he introduced me to them with this remark :

You must compliment Master Dittersdorf, not me. I had nothing to do with it.'

Whereupon they stared—and their staring did me good. One of them was Hubaczek, the famous French-horn player, who was in the service of the Field-Marshal and Master of the Ordnance, Prince Joseph Friedrich von Hildburghausen. He joined me on my way home—asked my name, where I lived, who was my father—and promised to call very shortly. He kept his word. After a few days he came, and stayed to dinner, when he told us that the gentleman in whose service he was had an efficient orchestra, which met for practice three mornings every week, at eleven o'clock. Would my father allow me to attend occasionally? The offer was gratefully accepted.

The very next day Hubaczek came to fetch me, and I took my violin. I was not a little surprised, when I came to the orchestral platform, to be offered the first desk.

We had hardly finished tuning, and were about to begin a symphony of Jomelli's which I knew already, when the Court composer, Bonno, stepped into the room. He had a yearly salary from the Prince for directing the grand concerts at Vienna, which were given all through the winter to the Austrian nobility. He stared at seeing a boy between eleven and twelve years old at the head of the band, and placed himself at my side to watch me. When the symphony was over he left the room, intending, I suppose, to report to the Prince, for both of them returned shortly afterwards.

The Prince called me to his side, and asked me very kindly who was my father, who was my teacher, how old I was, and so on. When I had given a plain, unembarrassed answer to all his questions, he went on to say :

'Are you able to play anything that is put before you *a vista ?*'

'If it is not too difficult,' I replied.

'Well, let us see!' said he, ordering Bonno to bring him from the cabinet an easy flute concerto and a sonata for the flute, the first of which I played off at once correctly enough. Some more symphonies and airs were tried, and then the solo was put before me. I got through it fairly well, though it was far harder than the concerto.

It was long past the dinner-hour, so the Prince, who was in very good spirits, kindly asked me to join his people at dinner, and told me to bring my father to him at five o'clock. They had a long interview in an adjoining room, and when he came back, the Prince said ·

'I think we both understand one another. We have only to see if your son is willing. Will you leave your father and come to me ?' he went on, turning to me. 'You shall want for nothing ; but, in return, you must work hard at music and languages. I will take care that you keep up your Latin, but your chief object must be to perfect your French and to learn Italian; that is indispensable for a musician. You will have plenty to do. I can't stand idlers. Would you like this? and will you promise me to work?'

I was dumfoundered, and fell on my knees.

'That I will, most gracious Prince!'

'Stand up, my son,' he said. 'In church you must kneel—before God—but not before me.'

'Keep your boy at home a few days longer,' he said to my father; 'but bring him back here on the first day of next month, when I will take him off your hands. For the future, he is to look up to me as his father.'

We were much touched when we took leave of the Prince, and my good mother wept for joy when we came home with the happy news. That same evening all our intimate friends were invited, that they might rejoice with us.

CHAPTER III.

I wear the *Prince's* livery.

ON the morning of March 1, 1751, my father took me to the palace of the Prince, in whose service I was, to start me on my new career. The Prince was not at home, and we were referred to the steward, Johann Ebert, a very dignified and respectable person, who had had orders to receive us. He was specially commissioned to look after me, and Bremer, Clerk of the Chancery, was to assist him ; so, after some words of advice, given in a very fatherly tone, he took me off to Bremer's room.

'You cannot speak to the Prince just now,' he said to my father, 'for he is out driving, and will not be home before two o'clock. You will dine as my guest at the official table, that you may see if your son can put up with our fare. As it is to-day, so it is every day.'

Then he showed me a list of rules for myself,

which, he said, the Prince, in his own person, had dictated to Bremer.

Bremer, a handsome man, about twenty-six years of age, welcomed my father very politely, and showed me my room, which adjoined his. Everything was new there — a neat bed, a writing-table, a chest-of-drawers with ornamental brasswork, comfortable chairs ; in short, a complete set of furniture. He handed me the inventory of the articles of furniture and dress, adding that he was under orders to look after everything from time to time. I was obliged to change everything I had on, and rig myself out in a brand-new suit. The coat and trousers I wore every day were dark gray, the waistcoat red. The suit was made of fine Dutch cloth, and the buttonholes, after the fashion of the day, were edged with silver lace. I found linen in abundance, not to mention white silk stockings, new shoes, silver buckles, all of the latest and newest *façon*. The Prince had ordered these things without my having had a hint of what was going on ; for the tailor, the shoemaker, and the seamstress had been told to work up their materials in my father's house, and I was to know nothing about it.

'That is the Prince all over,' said Bremer, when he saw how amazed I was. 'He delights

leadership

in surprising people by his kindness. I suppose you never dreamed of all these arrangements? Well, mind you keep everything neat and tidy, be a good lad, and you will do very well. Here is your own key; you are at liberty to go in and out whenever you like.'

I felt not a little pleased with myself, when the Court steward placed me in front of a large mirror, and I could get a full view of my new turn-out. Fine feathers make fine birds.

'It is close on eleven o'clock,' said he. 'Go into the music-room; the rehearsal is about to begin.'

I went in, and found most of the orchestra already assembled. One and all overwhelmed me with congratulations on my promotion to the office of Kammerknabe. I was now one of themselves   I was the happiest of mortals.

The symphony was only just over, when Madame Tesi appeared. Bonno had recently composed two airs for her, and she wanted to try them. Though now over fifty years of age, she was still good-looking and pleasant. Bonno, after placing the music on the desk, sat down at the clavicembalo, and Madame Tesi stood behind him. She had a full, clear contralto voice, and her fine singing completely carried me away. When the song was ended,

she sat down in front of the orchestra and talked
to the Kapellmeister.

' Madame Tesi would like to hear you play,'
he called out to me. ' Have you any music
with you ?'

' Yes,' I answered, and fetched a sonata of
Zügler's, in which Hubaczek accompanied me.

Tesi soon began to call out ' Bravo !' at every
successful passage, and afterwards 'Bravissimo!'
Then she asked to be introduced to my father,
and talked French to him for a little time.
After a few instrumental pieces, she went up
to the clavicembalo, and sang the second air—
an adagio. I had been charmed by her brilliant execution in the first instance, and I was
now so moved by the tenderness and sweetness
of her expression, that I thought music could
go no further.

At last the thrice-repeated sound of the
porter's bell announced the arrival of the Prince.
He went up at once to my father, beckoned him
to the window, and talked very graciously with
him for some time. Then he addressed me :

' Well, I hope you like your room and everything in it ! Work hard, and try to please me ;
but, above all, be sure to read your rules again
and again, and shape your life accordingly !'

Then he ordered them to bring his flute and

a concerto, and sat down and played. I cannot honestly say he was a great conjurer, though he played far better than I had expected. He kept time correctly, and had a very good lip. The rehearsal ended with his concerto, and he went in to dinner.

When I came to Herr Ebert, I found with him the Prince's page, a certain Baron Ende, and the Chief Superintendent of the Pages, a Saxon of the name of Göhrn, who also bore the title of Secretary. Ebert introduced me to him, adding that he was to give me lessons in Latin and French. ' Besides that, he is kind enough to teach you fencing. You will have to wait for your riding, dancing, and Italian lessons, until we go to Schlosshof, the Prince's country-place, which he visits every year at the beginning of June.'

' I had almost forgotten the most important thing of all,' said he to my father. ' Although our Prince is a Catholic (he was brought up an Evangelical, but became a Catholic under the influence of the late Empress Elizabeth), Lutherans and Protestants make up nearly the half of his Court, and amongst them are Göhrn, Bremer, and myself, who are to act as guardians to your son. But we are not given to proselytizing, and in order that you may be quite happy, the Prince has told us to engage a priest of your own way of thinking, who will be well paid for instructing your son in his faith. As you happen to have a worthy priest already under your own roof, it will be more agreeable to the Prince if he will undertake the duty.'

My father, delighted with this generous offer, declared that Father John would gladly do so without any salary, and in effect the worthy man came to me twice or thrice a week, until the time arrived for our migration to Schlosshof, when he received a *douceur* of nine ducats, and as many yards of black Brussels camelot as sufficed to make a new gown for him.

By this time my readers will have had a slight foretaste of the exalted and humane sentiments of the Prince, but later on they will be better acquainted with the incomparable goodness of this nobleman's heart. So I will at once pass on to the history of that excellent woman, Madame Tesi, as I cannot find a more suitable place for it.

CHAPTER IV.

History of Vittoria Tesi—The parrot and the Holy Inquisition—A Duke supplanted by a theatrical wig-maker.

VITTORIA TESI TRAMONTINI was born at Tesi. Tramontini was the name of her husband, and nothing is more common in Italy than for singers and dancers, even after their marriage, to resume the more familiar name of their maidenhood. In the flower of her age she was already the first singer and actress of her day in all Europe, and she kept up that reputation until late in life.

The Padre Metastasio was so delighted with her extraordinary power as an actress that he wrote his 'Zenobia,' 'Didone,' and 'Semiramide' specially for her. The most famous impresarios in Italy contended for her, paying such large sums that she amassed a considerable fortune. She was also summoned to Madrid, where she made her *début* with

Farinelli, the most famous *castrato* that ever lived. The King of Spain, as is well known, valued him highly, not only for his extraordinary musical gifts, but also for his varied intellectual attainments, and ended by making him a Minister of State and investing him with the Order of Calatrava. So charmed was Farinelli with Tesi's powers, that he frankly told the King that, as long as he lived, he wished to sing with her and with nobody else. She was therefore engaged for some years, till Farinelli, whose voice was beginning to fail him on account of his age, ceased to sing, and withdrew to Bologna. Tesi earned large sums of money in Spain, and after every new opera the King presented her with any amount of jewels and dresses—in a word, the bulk of her fortune was made in that country. At length, in Charles VI.'s time, she was summoned to Vienna, and engaged there at a lucrative salary.

I must tell my readers a story about Tesi. It shows how rampant fanaticism was in Spain while she was there.

She had bought a very valuable parrot in Naples, and trained it with incredible patience to laugh exactly like a man, and to answer all sorts of questions in the best Italian. I myself have seen this extraordinary bird.

Whenever the Prince wanted to amuse his friends at dinner, he ordered the cage to be sent for, and let the parrot have a field-day. It was rare good fun, for whenever the mistress giggled at a joke, the bird laughed also. This, of course, set off the whole company, and the bird was encouraged to laugh all the more, until there was such a frightful row that one would have thought the whole party, masters and servants, had just been let out of a mad-house.

Tesi had taken her pet with her to Spain, and his cage always stood in her reception-room. There was a large party one evening, attended chiefly by grandees, and the conversation happened to turn upon the parrot and his tricks.

'I suppose he can talk?' asked a Spanish noble.

'Oh yes!' replied Tesi. 'You shall hear him directly.'

She stood up there and then, and made the bird chatter about this, that, and the other. The Kapellmeister, a Neapolitan who had written the opera in which Tesi made her first appearance in Madrid, observed with a smile that, from the parrot's provincialisms, it was obvious he had got his learning in Naples.

'Oh, I beg your pardon!' said Tesi. 'He speaks Tuscan like the most distinguished citizen of Rome You may take my word for it. I will give you a proof at once, ladies and gentlemen.'

She rang for her maid, and told her to bring some biscuits. She had coaxed the parrot for a whole year with this bribe, and it never failed. The bird answered all her questions to admiration. He had been so carefully trained that he almost seemed to reason like a man. All the sensible people there complimented Tesi on the patience and skill which she had shown in educating her pet, but there were some fanatical idiots amongst the crowd, who murmured to each other that it was not canny.

Tesi, highly amused by this superstitious scare, asked her friends to arrange themselves again in a circle This done, she began a discourse, seasoned with plenty of her native wit—she wanted to put her company into a merry mood. She went on, until someone else was moved to make a pretty good joke; then she began to laugh, and gave the signal to her parrot, who laughed until he set everyone off. Just such a mad scene followed as I have before described.

A short time afterwards, two gentlemen took

their leave, saying they had business to attend
to. Whilst Tesi's servant was lighting them
downstairs with a torch (he happened to understand Spanish), he plainly heard one of them
say :

'You are quite right, my friend. We must
let the Grand Inquisitor know all about this,
and to-day too.'

The servant, not knowing what they were
talking about, took no further heed.

Next morning, two men appeared in the
anteroom, followed by two porters, carrying
a large basket covered with black cloth. Having
set the basket down, they asked to speak with
the mistress of the house. Tesi chanced just
then to be in the reception-room, feeding her
parrot.

'Ha! ha!' sang out the Black Cloaks. 'Is
that the parrot which so astonished your party
yesterday ?'

'At your service!' replied Tesi. 'Who are
you? What do you want ?'

We are servants of the Holy Hermandad,'
was the answer, 'and the Grand Inquisitor has
ordered us to give your parrot over to the
Inquisition.'

His mistress protested, but in vain. A dash
was made at the cage, which was solemnly

transferred to the basket and covered over
with the black cloth. Then the procession
moved off.

Tesi wept bitterly at losing her dear *amico*,
as she was wont to call him ; but mustering
up courage, she put on her things and drove
off to Farinelli to ask his advice   He told the
King at once what had happened, and grew
quite eloquent as he assured him that the
parrot's cleverness was perfectly natural.
Though the King finally yielded to his
argument and interposed in the bird's favour,
a week more elapsed before Tesi got back
her beloved *amico* out of the hands of the
Inquisition.

I now resume the thread of her own history.

She sang for many years at the Court Theatre
in Vienna, and was rewarded in Imperial fashion.
When nearly fifty years old she left the
stage, and determined to pass the rest of her
life in retirement. Prince Hildburghausen, an
old admirer of her brilliant gifts, then invited
her to become one of his household, at a proper
salary. She accepted his offer, but absolutely
refused to be paid, declining every present
which the Prince wished to make her. I do
not suggest for a moment that there was anything between her and the Prince except friend-

ship and their common love of art.   The sequel
will show this.

Tesi's character was above reproach.   She
was utterly unlike the ordinary run of operatic
singers.   I could tell many things that redound
to her honour, but will content myself with
the story of her marriage, which, at any rate,
will show her in no common light.   Wherever
she sang, she was accustomed to receive all
sorts of visitors, but she knew how to make
it very difficult for anyone to speak of love.
She had plenty of admirers, and the most
ardent amongst them was the Duca di N.
He happened to find her alone one evening,
and used his opportunity to make a formal
declaration.   Tesi gracefully and courteously
refused to have anything to do with him.   The
Duke, however, believing the refusal a mere
feint, became all the more importunate, and
promised more and more.   Tesi answered him
with such dignity, and was so conscious
of commanding respect, that the Duke was
abashed, and withdrew, never venturing again
to renew the attack.   His passion continued—
it increased every day—and the oftener he
saw and heard the charming creature at the
theatre, the more he loved.   He made a
confidant of one of his courtiers, who tried

to negotiate in his master's favour, but was so
sternly rejected that he, as well as the Duke,
was forced to realize the hopelessness of getting
at the lady by such means.

'I am determined to win,' said the Duke,
'even if I have to marry her before all the
world! To-morrow evening I will surprise her
with a formal offer of marriage; but take care
she knows nothing about it.'

Of course the supple courtier promised the
strictest silence; but, thinking to curry favour
with his future Duchess, he went off there and
then to Tesi, and imparted to her, in the most
sacred confidence, the great secret which was
weighing upon his mind.

But what did Tesi do? To be quit of the
Duke's importunities once and for all, without
coming to loggerheads, she summoned to her
aid, that same evening, the stage barber, a
good-looking man, and formally offered to
become his wife.

'If you will have me,' said she to the
delighted and astonished Tramontini, 'here is
my hand! We will be married straight off,
early to-morrow morning. I will give you a
good round sum of ready money. Deal with
it as you please; it shall be yours absolutely,
together with all the interest. I will do the

housekeeping, and look after your clothes and your furniture.   Besides that, one-third part of my present fortune, and anything I may add to it in the future, in money or the worth of money, shall be legally assured to you ; but I stipulate once and for all (and I shall not change my mind) that we live apart, though man and wife in law. . . . If, after this stipulation, you will give me your hand, we will be married to-morrow.   You shall have till to - morrow morning early for reflection.

It may easily be supposed that the delighted barber gave her both hands instead of one.   The very next day, at nine o'clock, the two drove off to the Bishop, to obtain his sanction ; the wedding was to be celebrated in the nearest parish church they could find.   The license was obtained without difficulty, on explanation, and they were married at eleven, after which the lawyer, who was waiting for them at home drew up a contract for them to sign and seal. The wedding breakfast over, Tramontini's goods and chattels were transferred to Tesi's quarters, and she counted out to her enraptured husband two thousand zecchini in hard cash.

The surprise and embarrassment of the Duke may well be imagined, when he came back in the evening, to see the transformed Tramontini, in his Sunday best, sitting familiarly beside his adored Tesi, and to hear from her own lips the solution of the fatal riddle. She did her task delicately, and he put a strong restraint on himself, so as to try and appear politely indifferent; but it was impossible to conceal the feelings of wounded pride. He bade her a haughty good-bye soon afterwards, and never came back again.

Tesi and her husband lived quite happily together. For many years they were in the Prince's palace, until His Highness returned to Hildburghausen and assumed the guardianship of the young Duke, who was still a minor. Age and infirmity prevented her from undertaking so long a journey; so she parted with her illustrious friend and remained in Vienna, where she died a few years afterwards. The property she left behind her amounted to nearly three hundred thousand gulden, of which her husband inherited one-third, by virtue of the contract. Who got the rest, I cannot say; but whoever it was, he had to pay her servants double wages as long as they lived, and to give them her wardrobe, to be divided in equal shares.

Sleep softly, glorious woman! Let me honour thy memory to my latest breath!

CHAPTER V.

My tutor, Trani—My humiliation at the hands of the
cripple, Matthes—The watch.

WE never weary of talking about our early
days, for the smallest incident seems of importance to us, as we look back ; but we must
not assume that every trivial matter will interest
the reader. Therefore, let me briefly say that
I was well looked after, and got the best of
everything. I had my regular place at the
household table, where seven meals were daily
served and partaken of by some thirty persons.
I took my supper of an evening by myself.
Besides maintenance, I received five gulden
thirty kreutzer, for pocket-money, every month,
and had to account to Herr Bremer for my
expenditure. One of the Prince's servants was
paid for curling my hair every morning. My
linen was well attended to. I can truly say of
the Prince that he treated me as his own son.

My father dined with us on the first day, and came to my room afterwards, to beg of me not to spoil my good luck by any bad conduct. He blessed me at parting. I kissed his hand with emotion, and he left me. I must own that I very soon recovered myself. I inspected my wardrobe, and admired it all once again, bit by bit. My special joy was the beautiful gala costume, made of superfine French cloth, and adorned with splendid silver lace—quite enough to drive my father out of my head, vain coxcomb that I was!

That very day I was summoned to the Prince, to be introduced to Herr Trani, my future violin master. I was to give him a taste of my quality. I can truly say that he showed great zeal in the discharge of his duties.

I lived for the next three months in the strictest obedience to my code of rules, which I read through again and again. It is a pleasure to look back upon the time. Shortly before that, when we were on the eve of starting for Schlosshof, my father arrived with the joyful news that the Prince had taken my eldest brother, Joseph, into his service, at a salary of three hundred gulden a year, exclusive of board and lodging, so that he was to go with us to Schlosshof. I could hardly contain myself for

joy, and knowing that my father was not averse
to a little glass of good Cyprus wine, once in a
blue moon, when he was in extraordinarily good
spirits (he would take my elder brother or
myself away to the Gewürzgewölbe at the
Grüner Kranz, now the Graben), I slipped a
thaler quietly into the hand of my servant,
a poor half-witted, bandy-legged fellow, and
ordered him to get a bottle, on the sly.

Meanwhile, my father, anxious to see what
progress I was making under my new teacher,
asked me to play something, and I chose a
sonata by Locatelli, out of an engraved collection which Trani had given me. These sonatas
may sound old-fashioned nowadays, but I would
earnestly recommend them to every beginner
on the violin—for practice, not for show pieces.
Once master of them, he will make great progress in fingering, bowing, arpeggios, double-
stopping, etc.

My father, in the exuberance of his spirits,
had determined on the Cyprus wine beforehand, and was highly pleased and surprised
to find it within reach. He was gratified by
my attention, and lingered a good while, giving
us friendly advice about Court life, interspersed
with many racy anecdotes. When he left us
in the evening, he presented me with a bright

Kremnitz ducat, to pay the reckoning, as he called it, besides giving my fool of a servant a gulden, with which he danced about on his twisted feet, half mad with joy.

These particulars would hardly have been worth recording in themselves ; but as I possessed the not very edifying gift of mimicking the oddities and weaknesses of other people, I was copying the servant on the following morning, dancing up and down the room with crooked legs, and Bremer, like myself, was in fits of laughter at the exhibition, when the original appeared on the scene, bringing in our breakfast. Naturally we laughed the louder, and I went on with my caricature, which the good fellow did not seem to notice ; but he bore me a grudge, and that very day I had to pay heavily for my unseemly amusement.

When I took it into my head to make a butt of him at the dinner-table, and, calling to mind that heroic deed wherewith I had already entertained the company in his absence, repeated the St. Vitus's dance of yesterday (for, though earnestly requested by those present, he declined to do so himself), at first he went off into a paroxysm of laughter. Afterwards, however, so soon as quiet was restored, he posted himself, with a plate under his arm, behind the chair of one of my companions, and said, with an air of meek simplicity :

'Well, young gentleman, I quite admire your cleverness! You have seen me but once at my antics, and you can hit them off to a turn. What a pity you are not so quick with your violin! But that is quite another matter. I am often sweeping out the passage when you are having your lesson. I hear your master showing you how to do the trick with some flourish, and you try to imitate it, and you come to grief hopelessly. Then he sings out " Da capo," but it is still no go, for after twenty or thirty scrapes, you make about as much music as two dozen cats mewing in chorus! By-the-by, Mr. Steward, I ought to have told you a week ago that since this young wag came to us '—here he pointed at me—' all the rats and mice have disappeared!'

'Well done, Matthes!' I interrupted 'Serve me well right! You have paid me out handsomely for my impudence.'

'For shame, Matthes!' said Ebert. 'You have shown once again that you are a rough, rude fellow, fit for nothing but to chop wood. Now you may see for yourself how to make it all square again with the Kammerknabe.'

'Don't be angry, young gentleman,' said

he, in the gentlest tone imaginable. ' It came out without my thinking. I meant no harm. Please forgive me.'

'With all my heart, my dear Matthes,' I answered. ' I not only forgive you, but thank you as well for the good lesson you gave me. Here are twenty kreutzers for you. Get some wine for yourself! You have made it all right.'

I was unexpectedly summoned to attend upon the Prince the next morning, and told to bring a sonata in which I had just been drilled by Trani. I went. Madame Tesi and Bonno happened to be present.

'Well,' said the Prince, ' I dare say you have often wondered that for the last eleven weeks I have not asked you to play me a note, but I thought I should see all the better how you had got on, and that is the reason. Now let me hear you!'

I played my sonata ; Hubaczek accompanied, and the Duke was pleased. He then made a sign to Hubaczek to withdraw, and I, thinking he meant me to go also, went towards the door.

' No, you are to stay,' said the Prince. ' Or are you sleepy already ?'

' Oh no, your Highness! It is quite early.'

' What is the time ?'

'I will look at the clock' (going to the door).

'Where are you off to again?'

'To the antechamber, to look at the clock.'

'Nonsense! Look at your watch!'

'My watch?'

'Yes.'

'I have not got one.'

'No watch?'

'No, your Highness.'

'And yet you have never missed your lessons. How did you manage that?'

'Whenever I wanted to know the time I went to the antechamber.'

'But that is ever so far off.'

'I have a good pair of legs to carry me.'

Well, to save going up and down stairs in the future'—here he presented me with a watch—'take this, and go to your room!'

I thanked the Prince, kissed his hand, and made for the door.

'By-the-by,' he called out; 'come back! Just a word! They tell me you can sing and dance prettily, and have had lessons from Matthes, the boots!'

The blood rushed to my face, and I was dumb.

'Never mind,' said the Prince. 'Your blushes show me you are ashamed, and I feel certain that you will take care not to blush for shame any more. However, I had far rather my people were quick and lively and on the spot ; no sleepy tortoises for me, that do not know how to help themselves! Of course you were wrong, but you mended the matter at once, and that showed you were *on the spot'* (he laid an emphasis on the words), 'and does you honour. Now go, my son.'

What a kind man he was! What delicacy he showed, even when making a present to a boy! I found out afterwards that I was indebted for my watch, not to my progress in music, but to the *savoir faire* which he made so much of. But it was as wise as it was considerate of him to leave me in that belief.

CHAPTER VI.

The journey to Schlosshof, and my first stay there—*Private shooting-guilds—Strolling players—Pergolesi's 'Serva Padrona'* in a coach-house.

In the beginning of June we moved to Schlosshof —the Prince, and all his Court with him. It was a glorious place in summer. The castle and the gardens were splendid, covering the area of half a town. It had been built, from cellar to roof—this Schlosshof—by the hero, Eugène of Savoy, who lives in the memory of every patriotic Austrian ; he proved his taste in architecture by the erection of the Belvedere Palace in Vienna, now the property of the Emperor. The beauty of Schlosshof may be taken for granted, when I add that Kaiser Franz was so delighted, that he bought the entire property from the Prince, and presented it to his great favourite, the Archduchess Christine.

Herr Trani, and Herr Pompeati with him, followed a few days later. The latter had been

a very distinguished solo-dancer in his early
days. When advanced in years, he left the
theatre, and gave lessons in dancing and in
the Italian language. He taught me and the
page, Baron Ende, both of these arts. Ende
became an expert in both ; that acted as a spur
to me, and I was soon abreast of him.

Trani brought me a very fine violin. The
Prince had purchased it for me through him.
Many people have urged me to sell this instrument, but I kept it by me until two years ago,
when I gave it to my eldest son.

My various lessons, riding included, were
continued daily, just as in Vienna. Baron
Beust, the Prince's equerry, and the Master
of the Horse, took it by turns to instruct me.
The page and I waited at table on alternate
days, and as Madame Tesi generally talked
Italian, I profited by this so far as to speak it
pretty well, within a few months' time. I was
limited to French, when I conversed with the
Prince, as he wanted me to have some practice.
If I stumbled now and then at a word, or went
wrong in grammar, he always corrected me very
kindly, and made me repeat the sentence. . . .

As the Prince was an ardent and very accomplished sportsman, both small and big game
was well preserved on his domain, though he

could not get about as well as of old, because
of his weak feet, and could not therefore satisfy
his passion for hunting.   His favourite diversion
was deer-shooting, for that could be carried on
when he was comfortably seated in a garden-chair.
But as no one went after the stags but he himself, Madame Tesi and Baron Beust, who did
not frighten them much, the game increased
too rapidly.   So the Prince ordered a target-
practice every Sunday afternoon, and seven of
the orchestra, Trani and my brother included,
had to attend it, and qualify for giving the too
venturesome stags a lesson.   I happened to be
present at the scene of action, on the very first
Sunday, and was so greatly delighted with the
manœuvres, that I expressed a wish to join the
shooting-party, whereupon the Prince sent for
No. 1 of Marcus Zellner's rifles out of the gun-
room, and condescended to give me a lesson in
priming and loading, sighting and aiming.   I
fired—pouf! and lo and behold, a bull's-eye!

'Bravo!' cried the Prince.   'You hit something besides your notes;' and he admitted me,
then and there, to the shooting-guild.

After that, we had plenty of shooting matches
on our own account.   We used to compete for
stockings and pocket-handkerchiefs.   I had my
share of the prizes.

I made similar progress in riding, and soon
I was allowed to go out of a morning with
Baron Beust, who was an excellent horseman,
and afterwards with the Prince himself. I was
in the Seventh Heaven. Besides this, there
was another amusement which seemed to me
the *ne plus ultra*. Here also, in this charming
place, in my careless, merry youth, I laid the
foundation of my future love for the theatre—
a love which never failed me in after-life ; and
here the modest gift that I had for dramatic
music was first encouraged.

One day, a certain Piloti, manager of a troop
of actors, drove up to the village inn, with his
wife and another actor, and asked to see the
Prince. On being introduced, he said that
he was acting in Pressburg from November
until the end of May, but that, in the summer,
he and a few of his company were on tour
through the smaller towns of Austria. Might
he venture to ask His Highness's permission to
come for a fortnight, and play before the Court ?

The Prince asked what sort of pieces he
could give. After mentioning a number of
comedies, he added that they were ready with
the ' Serva Padrona ' of Pergolesi ; it had been
performed over thirty times in Pressburg, by
general desire, and the house was crammed

every night. With his wife, and one actor, he could perform the Intermezzo that very day, and they had brought proper dresses expressly for the purpose. Although the other two were Germans, and the manager himself was only half an Italian, they all spoke with the best accent, for he had taken infinite pains to secure this. If His Highness would like to hear the piece to-day, it could be given in any room he chose ; all that would be wanted would be some folding-screens.

'With all my heart!' said the Prince, and sent off at once for the steward, ordering him to get ready the *sala terrena*, and to see that the three guests were well fed and looked after. The Intermezzo was tried with a few violins, for the sake of the *tempi*, and the play began.

The Prince, Madame Tesi, Bonno, and the whole orchestra confessed that the actors deserved great applause. When the music was over, the Prince and Piloti went into the garden together, and there they agreed for daily performances, at a certain price, from the first of July to the last day of October, exclusive of days forbidden by the Court. They selected for the temporary theatre a coach-house, built on so grand a scale by Prince Eugène that it had all the look of a *salon*.

Oh, the joy of that prospect for me! I waited, with a beating heart, for the arrival of the troupe, from whom I expected untold bliss. I counted the days and hours; it seemed to me that June would never end. My mind began to wander over my lessons; it was a good thing that Piloti only delayed a few days. He arrived with a company of eight persons, and put up his stage, which was really very pretty, and still so fresh that there was no sign of wear and tear, as there is too often, where strolling players are concerned.

The opening performance was on the first of July, and we had one every day until the end of October. The Prince, who never enjoyed any pleasure, unless it was shared by others, gave free admission, not only to everyone at Court and to the entire household, but to every stranger —even to the peasants, though these last were only admitted on Sundays and *fête*-days.

With all these varied amusements, which made my life at Schlosshof a Paradise, my studies went on uninterruptedly. So far from hindering, they encouraged me to work, and even if I gave no proof of fiery genius, which never slumbers and sleeps, and seldom does what it is told, I am just as well content; for my honest punctuality in time and business stood me in ood stead in later life.

CHAPTER VII.

I make my *début* in Vienna—A useful lecture for *virtuosi*—
Cadenzas—Criticism of Mozart's and Dülon's fantasias
by a nobleman of Vienna.

WE were back again in Vienna by the beginning
of November. My lessons were diminished
by two, for the riding and dancing were dis-
continued, so that I gained all the more time
for practising by myself. That is the chief
point with anyone who means to play well ;
as in music, so in everything else.

Trani told me that I must now hold myself
in readiness for a solo performance at every
Academy (the Viennese name for a concert).
The Prince gave these concerts to the nobility,
on Fridays, throughout the winter.

'Your pieces by Locatelli, Zuckarini, and
Tartini are well enough for practice, but not
for show ; besides that, they are too well known
here. You had better play Ferrari ; you know

already three of his concertos and four of his sonatas. But these will not be enough, so you must study new things meanwhile, and Ferrari's are quite the best for that purpose.'

Ferrari, the famous violinist, had come to Vienna two years before I entered the Duke's service. He used to live there for three-quarters of the year, and he was greatly admired and handsomely treated, not only by the Imperial Court and by the managers of theatres, but also by amateurs. I never heard him play, but his reputation in Vienna was very great in my time. I still remember his concertos and sonatas, which even now are deservedly praised. He and Trani became the closest friends, from the moment that he set foot in Vienna. Wherever Ferrari played, there was Trani to accompany him ; so powerful was Ferrari's influence, that Trani could repeat to a nicety his fingering, bowing, and delivery. In gratitude for his constant services as accompanist, Ferrari allowed him to copy his finest concertos and sonatas.

Though Trani had given up solo-playing for some years past, he still possessed the gift of making his pupils execute passages which were now beyond his own powers, and so it came about that I learnt the art of playing Ferrari's pieces just as their author intended. Many a man in Vienna used to call me *Ferrari's little ape !*

I was universally applauded on the first occasion of my playing before the great people, and my master was congratulated on all sides. Some went so far as to say that he had produced another Ferrari in me.

Next morning, however, at the usual hour for my lesson, I observed that he had something on his mind, for he did all sorts of things before beginning, which was his way when he had to read me a lecture. As I thought that the effect of yesterday's ovation would still be fresh, I could not make out his chilling gravity, and still less his complete silence on the subject of the applause bestowed on me.

' Have you any complaint to make against me ?' I asked.

' No,' he answered. ' My complaint is against your audience, if you wish to know.'

I was dumb.

' Do not be offended,' he continued ' You did honour to yourself, to me, and to the Prince, and for that matter I am thoroughly satisfied with you ; but give me your best attention, and please remember what I am going to say ! They applauded you, yes ! but, mind you, they only did so because you are still a child, and they expected less ability than they actually found. If you had been sixteen, you would not have been noticed at all, much less praised. Why, they told me, in your presence, that I had turned you out *a second Ferrari*—words that I regard not merely as an empty compliment, but as obviously untrue, for I tell you candidly that, so far, you are hardly a shadow of the great man. It is my duty to give you good wine,—and to nip premature conceit in the bud. That comes only too soon, and it makes young *virtuosi* intolerable. But I can promise you this, for I know better than anyone else what you can do—that if you work, up to your seventeenth or eighteenth year, as hard as you have done, you will justly deserve to stand by the side of a Ferrari. Study minutely the individual points of every artist, be he violinist, singer, or instrumental player, and when you have ascertained their various points of excellence, make them your own, not by slavish, but by *free* imitation ; above all, let your own feelings be your guide ; then you will be an artist. Now, my son, let us turn to our lesson !'

Trani had hitherto taught me his own cadenzas to the concertos and sonatas of Ferrari, but after bringing me a new concerto to study, he told me that I must now begin to invent them for myself.

And here I will interpose a remark.

Cadenzas—in old days they went by the name of capriccio—were at that time all the fashion, but only with a view of giving the *virtuoso* a chance of showing his skill in improvising offhand.   Later on, this was abandoned, probably because, through the awkwardness of the artist, all that was good in the performance of a concerto was spoiled when it came to the cadenza.   A new custom arose,—but I cannot bear it, except for the pianoforte, and in the hands of men like Mozart, Clementi, and other great creative geniuses, who—to display their rapid powers of invention by the medium of the so-called fantasia—pass on to a simple theme, which they vary again and again, according to all the rules of art.   Of course they have been imitated by a crowd of little apes, and now variations and fantasias are so common, that you never hear the sound of a piano at a concert without knowing that you will be regaled with every sort of twist and twirl and turn.   It is positively sickening to listen to beardless boys, breaking their necks over things which none but real masters should attempt!   One would rather cut and run than endure all these crude vagaries and *tours de force*.

How angry I was a few years ago with one, Dülon by name, when I heard him fingering away with his flute, on which, as my honest bandy-legged servant would say, he was making all sorts of 'tootles and twirligigs,' ending, *nota bene*, in variations without any sort of accompaniment. Meantime, just at the very moment when Kozeluch and I were mutually exchanging confidences over this infliction, we were interrupted by his Excellency, Count N. N., who graciously addressed us thus :

'Gentlemen, each of you is a dictator in music! Will you not both admit that music has reached its *highest* climax now ? Mozart sits down at a piano, and improvises with any number of harmonies. It does not want a conjurer for that, but for a flautist, with his poor thin instrument, to do the same! Surely that is wonderful?' ('Oh, oh!' thought I). 'How do you explain it, gentlemen?'

'Oh yes, wonderful indeed!' I replied, with a loud laugh, for just then I was thinking of Blumauer's description of the pretty music of Circe's suitors.

Kozeluch, however, put on the usual professional face, and said :

' " *O tempora ! O mores !* " '

The oddest part of it all was, that his Excellency understood neither my laughter nor Kozeluch's exclamation, but kept on repeating, again and again, that Kozeluch and Dittersdorf fully agreed with him.   Bravo !

To return to my history !

Gluck came to Vienna in the December of that same year.   The Prince's correspondent had informed him beforehand of the worthy man's great success in Italy, and he had received from him, only a few weeks since, the score of the well-known air, ' *Se mai senti spirarti sul volto*,' which had made such a *furore* in that country.   Mademoiselle Heinisch, a very famous soprano at Vienna, sang it by the Prince's orders, and everyone was loud in its praise. Naturally, after this, the Prince wished to know Gluck in person, and Bonno brought about an interview.   Gluck added to his knowledge of art a knowledge of the world besides ; he was well read, and was such a good talker that he soon became the intimate friend of His Highness.   A rehearsal was always held on the evening before the concert, so as to ensure a perfect and accurate rendering of all the music, and particularly of the new things ; and on these occasions Gluck, violin in hand,

appeared *à la tête* of the orchestra, which had
been strengthened as usual by a large number
of the choicest players.   No wonder that our
Academies were acknowledged to be the best
in all Vienna!

The ordinary singers were Madame Tesi, whom
we know of already, and Mademoiselle Heinisch,
a very lovely woman, with an exquisite soprano
voice   She had had offers of splendid theatrical
engagements, but these she steadily refused,
though a *douceur* would secure her services at
chamber concerts.   The Prince had engaged
her permanently for the winter.   Our tenor was
Herr Joseph Fribert, who had been educated
by Bonno, and was in the immediate service
of the Prince.   Our instrumentalists were
generally Herr Gentsch on the 'cello, Tüner
on the bassoon, Schmit on the oboe, as well
as the English horn, the two Hubaczeks on
the French horn, sometimes separately, sometimes *a due*, and finally, your humble servant.
Besides these, whenever any *virtuoso*, singer,
or player came to Vienna, and deservedly
succeeded in winning the applause of the public,
Bonno was ordered to arrange the terms, and
to secure him for the Prince.   The result was,
that we had Gabrieli, Guarducci, Mansoli, as
singers; Pugnani, and Van Maldre, on the violin;

Besozzi on the oboe; Le Claire on the flute; Stamitz and Leutgeb as soloists on the horn; and other eminent players.

Gluck had many of his symphonies and airs copied for the Prince, and every work from the pen of that worthy composer was a new and delicate morsel for us who listened.

Count Kaiserling, at that time Russian Ambassador, was an intimate friend of the household. One day, at dinner, they happened to be chatting *en ami* about music.

'By-the-by,' said Kaiserling, 'the twelve violin concertos, ordered from Benda of Berlin, have come at last.'

'Indeed!' said the Prince. 'And pray who played them?'

Kaiserling: 'A man of the name of Reinhard.'

Prince (to Bonno) : 'Do you know him?'

Bonno: 'Yes, Your Highness.'

Prince: 'What sort of man is he?'

Bonno · 'Well, he's no conjurer! I expect we have far better players here.'

Kaiserling: 'Do you think so? Why, I ordered the Precentor of the Cathedral here to send me his first violin, and I suppose he knows who is the best in Vienna!'

Bonno: 'Your Excellency should have asked for the best—not for the first. Of course

Reinhard is the first fiddle at St. Stephen's,
but he is not the best in Vienna.'

Kaiserling · 'Anyhow, Reinhard played off
a vista the six concertos which were put before
him, and in fine style, too !'

Bonno · 'You amaze me.   Benda's concertos——

Kaiserling : ' But they are not so hard as those
which he has arranged for himself; for I have
been commissioned by Prince N. of St. Petersburg to order these concertos in my own name,
not his, and so Benda addressed them straight
to me, and not to St. Petersburg.   I shall
despatch them by the next courier ; but '—ad-
dressing the Prince—' if it be Your Highness's
pleasure to hear them, order your band to get
ready, and I will order Reinhard.   We can
have six of the concertos this evening, and the
rest to-morrow morning.'

Prince : 'Why not the whole twelve to-
day ?'

Kaiserling : ' Impossible !   It would be too
much for Reinhard.   Yesterday, after playing
the first six at my house, he was so tired that
he had to stop.'

Prince : ' Well, that does make a difference.
I never thought of it.'

Count Kaiserling drove home after dinner,

and ordered Reinhard to wait on the Prince, to whom he played the first six concertos, that same evening. All of us, including even Bonno, Gluck, and Trani, were delighted, and certainly Reinhard played them with exquisite neatness and delicacy. I had only one fault to find, which was that he shirked every cadenza, and passed on at once to the shake.

I was told by Baron Ende, who was in waiting, that, on the following day, the Prince had talked over these violin concertos with Gluck and Bonno, and had praised Reinhard.

'H'm!' answered Bonno 'I would back Karl to have played them just as well.'

Prince : 'The deuce you would!'

Bonno : 'Yes, I warrant him.'

Prince (to a servant): 'Tell Karl to come to me!'

I came.

Prince (to me) · 'Do you like the Benda concertos?'

I : 'I do, Your Highness. They are uncommonly fine.'

Prince (smiling): 'Yes, and difficult too.'

I : 'I do not think so. The music lies so well to the hand.'

Prince · 'How can you say so, seeing you have not played a note of it?'

I: ' It would be ridiculous if I could not tell that, just from hearing them.'

Gluck: ' *Dice bene, ha ragione.*'

Prince: 'Would you venture to play the other six at sight ?'

I: 'Why not—if they are not harder than yesterday's ?'

Prince · 'What, if I were to send word to the Ambassador, that I could put another violinist in Reinhard's place ?'

I · 'If Your Highness pleases.'

Prince: 'Suppose you were to break down and disgrace me ?'

I · 'If I do, may the porter put me under arrest for a week, on bread and water !'

Gluck (to the Prince) : ' *Mi piace la presenza di spirito di questo ragazzo.*'

Bonno (to Gluck, with a laugh) : 'Why, the lad understands that, just as well as if you had said it in German !'

Gluck: 'Well, so much the better !'

The Prince sent a message to the Count then and there, and said to me :

' Now be off, and see that your violin is in order.'

I: 'Oh, it is always in order ! Herr Trani told me once for all, that no violinist should go to bed without having tried all the strings of his violin. If one of them be out of tune, the new one, which he puts on instead, will stretch in the night, and be all the better next day.'

Gluck smiled approvingly.

I went to my room, took my violin, and practised cadenzas as well in the major as in the minor key. Tram came upon the scene, and though he shook his head on hearing of my audacity, he gave me encouragement and urged me to spare no pains.

The music began. I played the other six concertos, which Reinhard had not yet attempted, as well as I could, and I brought in regular cadenzas wherever they were indicated. I gathered from the conversation of all my audience, amongst whom Gluck was the most emphatic, that they had not expected this, and were pleased. When I asked Trani if the Prince would allow me to play the other six concertos as well, he said :

'If only you do not spoil the good effect of the first with the last !'

However, as I insisted, he went off to the Prince, muttering, '*In nome di Dio !*' and I did play them ; they seemed to me twice as easy.

I do not care to repeat what was said, for I should be accused of singing my own praises. But I ask any unprejudiced person who it was that really deserved the praise. Why, my master, of course, who took such honest pains with me, and especially the kind gentleman who spent so much on me, and took such an interest in my education! And yet, my excellent benefactor——But I am anticipating.

So far so good, but, as usual, my good master gave me a little sermonette the next morning.

'Honour to whom honour is due!' said he. 'You came off very well yesterday. I congratulate you sincerely; but — but you may play these tricks once too often. I have seen many an excellent *virtuoso* lose his reputation over that sort of thing. You may thank your stars that you came off with a sound skin. Fancy, if one of your strings had snapped just a few bars before the arpeggios, which occur in almost all twelve concertos! How could you have managed arpeggios for four strings on three strings only, in a concerto in which I have not drilled you, or how could you have extemporized variations? Of course you would have stuck fast. To be sure, I have always trained you, in your exercises, to look out for the three-strings emergency; but when you are playing at sight, by the devil! it's a different matter altogether. I hope you do not think me unkind?'

In fact, it was an invariable rule with my wise and far-seeing master to make me repeat on three strings any concerto which I had thoroughly mastered, and this practice often stood me in good stead in the after-years of my professional career.

The Prince used to go often to Court, generally in the forenoon. On one occasion, he returned with the news that the Emperor had promised to visit Schlosshof for a few days in July, bringing the Empress and some of the eldest Grand-Dukes and Grand-Duchesses with him; so he determined to remove thither himself at the beginning of April, instead of June, in order to make fitting preparations for the entertainment of his distinguished guests. Several extra hands were taken on—an engineer, a painter, a carver, and so on. Five more players were added to the band—a double-bass, a cellist, and three violinists, of whom my younger brother, Alexander, was one, for he was already a good orchestral player. The Prince gave him a place at the household table, and increased my elder brother's pay by a monthly addition of twelve gulden, in return for which he was to give Alexander further instruction on the violin, clothe him, and share his room with him. My father, however, undertook to pay for his clothes.

CHAPTER VIII.

Demoiselle Starzer—Thérèse Teiber—*Preparations*
*P*easants' ballet—The story of the four bagpipes.

B Y the time of our arrival at Schlosshof, the
place was already swarming with professionals
and artists, carpenters, joiners, painters, lac-
querers and gilders ; one was always rubbing
up against busy people, toiling and moiling
here, there, and everywhere, for the grand folk
who were expected.

Bonno had long ago been commissioned by
the Prince to write music for two plays by
Metastasio ; Gluck too had undertaken to set
that poet's 'Ballo Chinese,' and had only deferred
doing so, because the author had been asked by
the Prince to rearrange the libretto, introducing
a man's part in addition to those of the three
women. Gluck, therefore, did not arrive on the
scene before the middle of May. Besides the
usual troupe of singers, there was also a certain

Mademoiselle Starzer, a sister of the famous ballet-writer of that name, whose works had been greatly admired, and had brought him in large sums of money, not only in Vienna and Paris, but also at St. Petersburg, where he had lived eight years and more. The lady had a deep contralto voice, and sang splendidly. Bonno was her master. We know what that means. He had an extraordinary gift for teaching singers, and I could quote the names of many of his pupils as a proof of what I say. I confine myself, however, to one—that of the great vocalist, Thérèse Teiber, who created an unprecedented sensation in Vienna, Dresden, and London, and even in Italy as well.

As the time for the Imperial visit drew nearer, we worked harder and harder, and the operas were rehearsed very frequently. Amongst other spectacular pieces, the Prince had ordered a *fête* in honour of Bacchus, which was to include a comic interlude, a ballet, and a *Cuccagna*. Country lads and lasses were to figure as carpet-knights, dancers, and satyrs. Twenty-one couples had to appear in the ballet, which was designed and composed by Pompeati, and forty persons about the Court were ordered to study it, in order to drill the rustics in the many and really intricate mazes of the dance. So each of those, who were told off to rehearse either the men or the women, took a boy or a maiden, and danced and danced all over the place, until everyone knew the figures by heart. Though this went on day after day, it took us over three weeks to learn our lesson. We danced to a simple tune, which was played at rehearsals on a solitary violin. This was my own arrangement; Pompeati, our ballet-master, had hummed it to me and given me the *tempi*.

One day, when we were rehearsing, the Prince said, 'We must be thinking about an orchestra; it ought to be as funny as the ballet. May I ask every member of the band to favour me with his opinion?'

Even Gluck and Bonno were consulted. One proposed this, another that. When it came to my turn, and I had to give my vote, I said that I had ridden last year with Baron Beust to the village called Hof an der March, and on arriving there, had fallen in with a wedding, and heard two bagpipers, who were accompanying the dancers. The larger bagpipe, usually called the *polnischer Bock*,* was an octave lower than the small one, and one melody was played on both instruments. How would it be, if we were to scour all the neighbouring villages for bag-

* *Bock* means also a he-goat.

pipes, great and small, and press them into the service? We should be sure to find four out of the lot which would tune together; and these would be enough to fill the whole courtyard.

'Yours is the best plan of all,' said the Prince. 'But I am afraid that the fellows will not be up to playing the same melody.'

'No fear of that,' I replied, 'for the melody twice repeated is not more than two-and-thirty bars long'

'Good!' said the Prince. 'Please see to the matter for us.'

When the ballet rehearsal was over I ordered the steward to send off an express there and then to every village, and get together every bagpipe and *polnischer Bock* that could be found on the estate. There was to be a grand meeting at the village hostelry that evening, at five o'clock. The order was so well attended to, that, by the time appointed, I had got together over a dozen bagpipe *virtuosi*, and was so successful as to find two small and two large instruments perfectly in tune together. These I kept, and dismissed the others. Then I got my own violin, and dinned the melody again and again into the ears of the four pipers, until they had it perfectly by heart. That settled, I ordered them to stay where they were for the night,

until I came to fetch them betimes next morning.

At 5 a.m. next day (for the ballet rehearsal
began at 5.30) I ran to the inn, found my four
windbags, and made them rehearse the melody
again, until it went to my satisfaction. Then I
bade them follow me, and after ranging them
behind one of those wings of the castle which
formed the courtyard, I told them to keep quite
quiet until they were called.

At last the Prince came to the rehearsal, and
addressed me thus :

' Do not forget my orders about the bagpipes !'

' That is all done, Your Highness,' I
answered.

' Where are they ?' said he.

' I will bring them at once.' And I ran off
hastily round the corner.

' Now, come along !' I shouted to the pipers,
' and blow like blazes behind me !'

So said, so done. They puffed and blew
with such savage energy, that the Prince heard
the melody ever so far off. As we came round
the corner, I let myself go triumphantly, and
jumped about in front of the procession like a
billy-goat. Seeing my antics, the idiots thought
they must do the same, and each one hopped

along behind me like mad.   This amused me
so much, that I redoubled my tricks to imitate
them, and the funnier I was, the funnier they
became, trying to imitate me.   Their zeal knew
no bounds.   In short, the five mad musical
goats made the Prince laugh till he cried, whilst
the ballet-dancers shouted in chorus, and everyone bleated all round.

‘ Bravo, Mr. Merryman !’ said the Prince, in
great delight.   ‘ You have done your part well;’
and he felt for his purse, and presented me with
six bright ducats.

Then we went on with the ballet, and after
five or six rehearsals, the bagpipes and the
peasant dancers got on capitally together.   In
short, everything was going as well as possible.

I had another commission to execute later on ;
it seemed more arduous than the last, but I
scored another success.

We were rehearsing Bonno’s drama, ‘ Il Vero
Omaggio,’ and the Prince said he thought it was
a pity that the last verse should not be repeated
by a chorus.

‘ You may be right,’ replied Bonno · ‘ but
where are we to get the singers ?’

‘ I have five parishes on my estate,’ said the
Prince, ‘ and that means five schoolmasters as
well ; probably each one has boys and girls,

besides an assistant; surely we could easily get together twenty chorus singers.'

'Forty would not be too many for our stage,' answered Bonno.

'Well, if the worst comes to the worst, we can get them from Pressburg at the last moment. Meantime, I will give Karl a commission to teach the schoolmasters and their underlings their business.'

I got my commission, and managed everything so well, that the Prince had no need to summon his singers from Pressburg, as we shall see later on.

The necessary arrangements for the reception of the Imperial Family were now complete. To ensure safety and good order, the Prince asked the commanding officer at Vienna to send him two companies of infantry and one squadron of cavalry. Forty foot-soldiers kept guard, and the horsemen were told off for the spectacular performances which were to be given in outlying places; they were to patrol the district for four days and nights continuously, and also to act as firemen. The little brigade encamped on the Hutweide.

CHAPTER IX.

The Emperor Francis at Schlosshof—Chorus of two hundred peasants, some of the singers seated in the trees—Water-*fête* — The swimming garden — Chinese opera by Gluck—Splendid *mise-en-scène*—Departure of the Imperial Family.

THE eventful day was ushered in gloriously by the most perfect weather, and the noble guests with their suites, consisting of minions of high degree, reached Schlosshof at one o'clock. The Emperor, the Empress, the Archduke Joseph, the Archduke Charles, the Archduchesses Mariane and Christine, were all there; Prince Salm, the Mistress of the Robes, and six other gentlemen and ladies, were of the suite; they did not bring many servants.

The grandees made no formal entry; there were no triumphal arches, no volleys of mortars and cannon, no blaring trumpets nor shouting. The Prince had forbidden all parade, in order to enhance the surprise of the other fine sights. He received the visitors at the principal gate, attended only by Hofcavalier Beust.

After luncheon, the guests drove to Nieder-wenden, and when the Prince had shown them all over it, he set them down at an open-air theatre, with a noble view of the blue mountains of Pressburg in the background. Then, when the overture to the play began, a crowd of peasants pressed forward ; some of them kept at a distance, others clambered up the trees, to the great amusement of the Emperor. How surprised and delighted he was, when all the peasants—men, women, youths, and maidens, either standing in a circle or perched on the boughs of the trees—broke out into a chorus of over two hundred voices, and repeated the last strophe of the drama, whenever it occurred, with such correctness and purity of intonation, that they might have been taken for professional singers. This was so extraordinarily effective that everyone was struck, and the Emperor grew quite emotional.

The Emperor was naturally simple and unconventional, full of delicacy and kindness. Seeing the Prince about to withdraw, to change his dress, he good-naturedly interposed :

‘ Pray stay as you are, Prince—and I shall be

obliged if you will let me be as I am, for if
not, I shall be the only person unadorned in the
company, and everyone will think me eccentric.'

The Empress added, with all her husband's
kindliness :

' Do keep on your pilgrim's coat, if you want
to be thought my particular friend !'

It would weary my readers were I to make a
long yarn about all the many *fêtes*, fireworks,
Bacchanal scenes, and hunting-parties which
were the order of the day; but I cannot help
a word or two before leaving the subject for
good, because, in the sad circumstances of my
present condition, it cheers me up to let my
fancy dwell on these scenes of my merry youth,
and I think I can promise myself that it will
please my readers too. What is every biography
but the tale of a journey in a foreign land?
Now and then it is pleasant to get rid of the
guide, and to talk about other things for a
change.

So I mean to tell all about a water-*fête*, given
on an artificial lake at Kroissenbrunn, which
had been planned by Prince Eugène, and walled
round with large blocks of freestone, by his
orders. It was eighty feet broad and a hundred
long. From bank to bank, in the centre of the
lake, two galleries were thrown across; on each

of these were seated a number of trumpeters and drummers, with other players on wind instruments; they were heard playing alternate strains.

In the lake itself, at a little distance from the shore, there stood, at regular intervals on each side, eight pedestals, painted so as to look like stone, and adorned with bronzed grotesques. On the first two pedestals, two live bears stood opposite each other, dressed as clowns; on the second two, two wild-boars, dressed as columbines; on the third, two big goats, dressed as harlequins; and on the fourth were two huge bulldogs.

You may fancy the noise made by growling bears, grunting pigs, bleating goats, howling dogs, and the music going on at the same time! All the masqueraders stood in the attitudes that best became their parts.

The picturesque hills, on both sides of the lake, were thronged with some thousands of spectators. Opposite the fishing-cottage stood a gallery, resting on pillars, with railings through which you could look. It was a wooden construction, but Quaglio, the famous stage architect, properly called '*il Bibiena redivivo*' ('the great architect, Cavaliere Bibiena, restored to life'), had so disguised it with a coat of paint, that anyone, looking at it from a distance, would have taken it for stonework.

After allowing his guests an interval in which to enjoy the scene, the Prince waved his handkerchief as a signal, and the show began.

Two gondolas emerged at either end of the gallery, and made towards the cottage; each was manned by four gondoliers, dressed in Venetian fashion. One of them sat on the beak of the vessel, with a bundle of spears, lances, and similar weapons, laid crosswise before him; two others rowed, and the steerer, turning the gondola wherever he chose, sat behind them. These two gondolas advanced, circling in different ways round the pedestals; they were afterwards joined by two others, then by two more, and then the last two. The eight went through their manœuvres with such accuracy, that no ballet-master, marshalling his *danseuses*, could have improved upon them. When they had gone their rounds, they were ranged face to face, and a tournament began, in which each water-knight, seated on the beak, broke from four to five lances; then they went once more round the pedestals on which the comic actors stood. At one and the same moment, each knight, armed with a staff, struck at one of the grotesque masks, a spring gave way under the blow, and a trap-door fell. Numbers of white ducks and geese, and one swan as well, were concealed in each of the hollow pedestals, and you may fancy the alacrity with which these winged creatures took to their native element, though a marionette rode upon each of them. These marionettes were various figures, proportioned to the size of the birds which they bestrode—clowns, harlequins, Anselmos, Doctors, Leanders, Pasquins, Scaramouches, and other Carnival mummers.

A fray ensued, and the knights seized their clubs and threatened one another. The gondolas darted about in studied disorder. When one collided with another, the knights dipped their clubs, which were hand-syringes, into the lake, and squirted their enemies. Whenever they neared a pedestal, the creature on it got the whole benefit of a shower-bath, and the animals loudly resented the rudeness of the whole proceeding. The effect on the audience may be imagined, for orders had been given to the musicians on either bank to blow in any key they chose Directly after the skirmish had begun, one trumpeter blew a shrill blast in D, whilst another, with the aid of a crook, did the same in C, and another in E *la fa*. Some of the drummers had tuned up, others had tuned down ; oboists, clarinettists, bassoon-players, followed suit.   What an infernal discord it was ! The beasts growled, the ducks and geese quacked and spluttered, coming into collision with the moving gondolas every moment, and the three thousand spectators roared with laughter.   Show me the hypochondriac who could remain unmoved by such a spectacle!

When the scene had lasted long enough, the gondolas withdrew, and to the astonishment of all the spectators, the gallery was metamorphosed into a willow grove.   Laughter died away on their lips.   Even the chorus of animals and birds, who now beheld their tormentors vanishing in the distance, went out in a *diminuendo* in spite of the efforts of the Kurfürst of Mannheim's orchestra (which was then very famous for this sort of thing).   Everyone was on the *qui vive,* and staring at the magic grove, in eager expectation of the wonders about to be revealed there.

From the centre of the grove there slowly rose a pretty little garden, which looked like a floating island ; it went on moving, as though of itself, for about a quarter of an hour, towards the fishing-house.   It was fenced all round with palisades, painted white and green, half the height of a man.   The garden was planted with regular borders of box, within which flourished all sorts of most lovely flowers that happened to be in bloom just then. Between the borders were vases, painted white and green, containing twelve pomegranate and orange trees, laden with ripe fruit. In the middle of the garden was a round basin, filled with shoals of little bleak. A small dolphin, too, was seen disporting himself, and throwing up a jet of water. That was not all. At the end of the garden was Parnassus, with the winged Pegasus. At the blow of his hoof, two streams bubbled out to the right and left of the rocks, and fell into the basin by means of a little canal.

Baron Beust, dressed as a gardener, and Mademoiselle Heinisch, as a gardener's wife, stood at the entrance. The lady wore a white and green satin dress, covered with real flowers. The gardener had a gilded rake, and the lady a gilded watering-pot.

Two fishermen and fisherwomen, dressed in white and sky-blue satin, stood near the basin. I represented one, the second was my younger brother, and Mademoiselle Heinisch the younger and my sister took the women's parts. Each of us had a small draw-net, with a handle of black fretted wood, the nets being composed of thin silver lace.

When the garden had reached them, the royal guests were invited by the gardener to enter and pick the flowers. They gathered several nosegays, and the Archdukes and Archduchesses, to whom we had handed the nets, drew fish out of the basin, and threw them into the lake. At last they sat down on the benches provided for them, along the palisade. The gardener and his wife retreated to Parnassus, where there were plenty of ices, which they handed round in the most dainty glasses.

I shall never forget the scene—the mild summer evening, the grateful coolness after the glaring heat of the day, the soothing music of the wind instruments, the happy faces all around, and the graciousness and kindness displayed by the good Prince to everyone, the humblest guest included.

I still have before my eyes the exquisite performance of ' La Danza,' the slight comic opera, arranged by Metastasio from his play ' Il Ballo Chinese,' and set to music by Gluck. Quaglio's decorations were quite in the Chinese taste, and transparent. Workers in lacquer, carpenters and gilders, had lavished all their resources upon them, but their chief brilliancy depended on prismatic poles of glass, which had been polished by Bohemian craftsmen, and were carefully fitted into one another in empty places, previously soaked in coloured oils. They were very effective, even in sunshine and the broad light of day, but no pen can describe the surpassing and astounding brilliancy of these prisms when lit up by innumerable lamps. The reader must imagine the reflected brilliancy of the azure-coloured meadows of lacquer, the glitter of the gilded foliage, and, lastly, the rainbow-like colours repeated by hundreds of prisms, and flashing like diamonds of the finest water. The most vivid fancy will fall short of the real magic. And then, Gluck's god-like music! It was not only the delicious playfulness of the sparkling symphony, accompanied now and again by little bells, triangles, small hand-drums, etc., sometimes singly, sometimes all together, which at the very outset, and before the raising of the curtain, transported the audience : the music was from first to last an enchantment.

When the piece was over, the Emperor and the Prince left their seats, and asked that the curtain might be raised again, which was done. The monarch, opera-glass in hand, stepped on to the stage, and Quaglio explained to him every detail. He asked for a fragment of one of the prisms ; a hatful was brought to him, and he carried off three or four pieces. Then he entreated the Prince to be allowed to summon a draughtsman from Vienna, to make a drawing of the scenery. Quaglio, however, undertook the business, and finished his sketch on the following evening. The Emperor rewarded him with a handsome gold watch and chain.

In the following winter, the Emperor ordered a performance of the play in the Hoftheater near the Burg (the present National Theatre), and the *mise-en-scène* caused a great sensation in Vienna. I have often seen the play there, but in all honesty I must own that the staging was very inferior to that at Schlosshof, though the colouring was the same, after the same design, and they used the very same prisms. I cannot account for the fact. Besides this, the actors, except as singers (they had the great Gabrieli and others of equal merit among them), were not to be compared with ours—they had not been trained by Tesi.

The six days of feasting and revelry were over; the guests returned to Vienna, highly delighted with their entertainment. The Emperor ordered the Paymaster-General in Vienna to grant the officers of the little brigade a month's salary on their return, and a similar gratuity was given to the under officers and

private soldiers.   The Empress presented Tesi
with two bracelets, valued at two thousand
gulden, containing portraits of the Emperor and
herself, set in brilliants.   Baron Beust received
from Prince Salm a gold snuff-box, with a lid of
brilliants.   Mesdemoiselles Heinisch and Starzer
were given magnificent dresses ; Gluck and
Bonno had a gold snuff-box apiece, containing
a hundred ducats.   Twelve hundred ducats were
distributed amongst the servants and huntsmen.

To prevent any complaint as to favouritism,
the Prince ordered the Treasurer to pay according to the rate of wages.   He was just
going, when the Prince called after him : ' Karl,
poor fellow ! will get too little, with his two
hundred gulden ; you had better reward him
as if he earned four hundred.'

When the people moved off, it was discovered
that four horses, decked in the Imperial harness,
had been left, tied by their tails to the manger,
and it was currently believed that the grooms
had forgotten their charge in a drunken fit ; but
on closer examination, a paper was found
attached to each horse's cloth, on which the
Emperor himself had written :

' *Ces quatre chevaux, mon cher Prince, sont
de ce moment à votre disposition.*—François
Premier.'

The Prince had the horses led out, and when the cloths were taken off, everyone praised their beauty and their splendid appointments. The present was worthy of an Emperor of the Romans and of a Prince of Sachsen-Hildburghausen.

We resumed our ordinary life, after a lapse of three months, with this difference, that the Prince received many more visits from the neighbourhood and from Vienna. On such occasions there were frequent repetitions of the new operas, both at Niederweiden and in the theatre.

CHAPTER X.

I change my position—First efforts at composition—The
professore di violino—My venture before the desk—
White and red cheeks.

ON our return to Vienna, the Prince occupied
another palace, and in consequence of this,
alterations were made in the establishment and
in the band, to accommodate the household.
My brothers were quartered in the palace. My
monthly pay was thirty-seven gulden thirty
kreutzer; but the youngest of us, Alexander,
whom I was specially to look after, got twenty-
five gulden. At the same time, I was dispensed
from all the menial duties hitherto put upon me,
and was absolved from wearing a uniform. I
had managed my savings very well, and was
allowed to add to them by the sale of my old
clothes, so that I was able to get myself neatly
fitted out.

The Prince had sold the property of Schlosshof very advantageously to the Emperor, who had taken a fancy to it. His income having considerably improved, the establishment was enlarged, and we remained permanently in Vienna.

My French and Italian lessons came to an end, for I could talk both languages fluently; but I still worked at the violin, and Trani, who now lived at a distance, came every day, in one of the Prince's carriages, to give me a lesson.

One day, he told Bonno that he thought he had discovered a natural turn for composition in me, for my cadences, which were well thought out and original, disclosed some creative power. Bonno, who shared his interest in my gift, such as it was, offered to give me lessons in composition gratis, and, much to my satisfaction, he said that I might go to him three times a week. I kissed his hand with effusion. The prospect was too delightful.

At my first visit, he presented me with Fux's 'Introduction to Composition,' which in those days was reckoned one of the best works of its kind. It is written in Latin, and consists throughout of dialogues between a teacher and his pupils. I came across the book afterwards, translated into German. When Bonno handed me the volume, he said

' I assume you understand Latin ?'

After turning over a leaf or two, and examining a passage here and there, I answered :

' Why, it is such dog-Latin that any fellow in the second class could understand it !'

' Oh, indeed !' he replied, in his usual schoolmaster tone. ' We don't want elegant Latinity here, but good sound theory—and that the book contains. That's what we want !'

Of course he was right.

I had had a few weeks' instruction, when Bonno ordered me to compose a sonata on my own account. I wrote it, and brought it to him. After improving some notes in the bass, he asked me to try my hand at a concerto. This I accomplished in a fortnight's time. The scoring of a number of parts, however, was a sore difficulty, for not only did I come to grief often over the laws of thorough-bass, but I violated the golden rule, that the voice should not be smothered nor drowned by the accompaniment. My teacher pointed out every fault to me, explaining his reasons, and suggesting a method for improvement, after my many blunders. Four lessons were required before I got it right. That accomplished, he said :

' Now study the principal theme under Herr Trani's supervision. Write out the parts from the score, and when you have everything in good order, let the Prince hear what you have done.'

I played my concerto ; but how can I paint the intense happiness of hearing my poor work rendered, for the first time in my life, by a large and first-rate orchestra? I swam in a sea of delight. Anyone who has been in my position will know what it all means, and smilingly remember the impression of lofty independence, after his first emancipation. With all the pride of the poet, who sees his first successful song working wonders in a volume with silver clasps and edges, I stepped down from the platform where I had subjected the first effort of a mind, that was still far from having cleared up its own difficulties, to the criticism of such a crowd of *savants*, critics, and amateurs. I felt as if I were taller by several inches.

I was stimulated, by my not unsuccessful attempt, to prosecute my studies in pure counterpoint with all possible earnestness and zeal, but the harder I worked, the more numerous were the difficulties I encountered. Still, I was not to be frightened. Young as I was, I soon realized the fact that, however profoundly versed a composer may be in the rules of musical science, he cannot dispense with the qualities of *taste* and *imagination*, still less with the one thing needful—creative *genius*. This, although it is Nature's gift, and is only bestowed upon a few, needs unwearied industry and cultivation. Failing these, it shoots up like a wild-flower, and is barren of all results. So I resolved not only to listen to every novelty *con tanto d'orecchio* (this is the Italian equivalent for 'rapt attention'), but to find out why a beautiful thought is beautiful. And how often I discovered that it was beautiful, simply because it was in the right place, so that, if it had occurred elsewhere, it would either not have been remarked at all, or have spoiled the whole work.

The winter concerts came to an end after Easter, and all the summer was a holiday. To be sure, we were ordered to hold ourselves in readiness daily up to four o'clock, but if no order had arrived by that time, everyone was free to do as he pleased.

One day, when I knew that the Prince, Tesi, and Bonno were dining together at the Venetian Ambassador's, I went off on a country excursion, to see the grape-gathering. At that time, I was a passionate lover of billiards. I was like the good Emperor, and thought every day lost on which I did not play a game. So I returned to the coffee-house about a quarter to six o'clock, and the marker met me, calling out :

'It is lucky for you that you have come! The Prince has sent a courier here three times to fetch you. There is to be a concert at six o'clock at the Embassy ; all the rest of the band is there already. You are the only one missing.'

I rushed home, dressed as fast as I could, sent for a cab, and was in the ante-chamber at a quarter past six, where I heard the same story, about the Prince having sent for me three times. As soon as he was told that we were all there, we were summoned to the concert-room. I saw plainly, by his dark and scowling look, that I was in for a regular preachment next morning.

The concert began with a symphony, and as Trani was unwell, and could not lead the orchestra, I acted for him. The Ambassador was amazed at my performance, but still more so, when his wife sang an air which I never could have heard, and I took the *tempo* quite correctly. There was nothing wonderful about it, for when Bonno played the first few bars on the piano, I caught it up, just as any other person would. But when the song was over, the Ambassador went to the Prince and made a great fuss about the way I led, adding that he was a good judge, for although a dilettante, he was himself a *professore di violino.*

'Well,' remarked the Prince, 'when his time comes, you shall hear him play a solo; then you, who thoroughly understand such matters, will be enabled to judge whether he has any chance of becoming a *virtuoso.'*

I had heard every word, and thought that I should sink into the earth from terror, for, in my hurry, I had forgotten to bring a concerto or a sonata with me. I racked my brains for some device to get out of the dilemma gracefully, without being forced to confess that I had been careless enough never to think of such a thing—a fault the Prince never forgave, and was the less likely to forgive, that he had good reason already to complain of my being late. At last, after much consideration, I adopted a bold expedient.

'If I have to play a sonata,' said I to my younger brother, 'you must help me out of the scrape. Play some accompaniment in G, out of your head; never mind missing a note here and there! We can't help it.'

'All right,' my brother answered. 'Never fear! We shall not break down.'

My heart went up with a bound.

6

At last I **got** the dreaded order to play. With the utmost coolness, I walked to a table upon which some scores were lying, and took two parts from the first symphony that came to hand, the first violin part and the bass, one for myself, the other for my brother. Unfortunately, it was the symphony in E *dur*. In spite of that, I started energetically with my sonata in G. But I had hardly played ten or twelve bars, when I saw the Ambassador rise from his chair, and beckon to another Italian gentleman in passing. They both stepped up behind me. Imagine my misery, when it dawned upon me that the *professore di violino* was looking over my shoulder! To make matters worse, he took a very superfluous opera-glass, with which to stare at my music.

'Here's a pretty kettle of fish!' I whispered to my brother.

I resolved to make a clean breast of it, directly I had finished the first movement, and to beg the Ambassador not to betray me to the Prince. I soon found out, however, that Mr. Ambassador was not only no professor of the violin, but a mere empty windbag, who did not know a note, and only wanted to palm off his fictitious knowledge on his neighbours by saying, always at the wrong moment :

'*Adesso viene un passaggio !*' ('There is such a passage coming !')

Hearing this, I was rascal enough to extemporize a scale, flourish, or variation, and often with conspicuous success. The moment I saw that I was out of danger, my spirits rose. I played through my sonata with unwonted precision, and everyone was pleased. The Ambassador applauded me, and could not say enough in my favour to the Prince, congratulating him on the glorious acquisition he had made in me. Meanwhile, Bonno came up to me, and said ·

'You did very well to-day, you played with wonderful execution ; but I shall have to pitch into your brother for accompanying so badly.'

'Please do not !' I answered, 'for he was playing the bass by heart.'

'What do you mean ?' asked Bonno. 'Surely he had the music on his desk before him ?'

'That was all a sham,' I replied ; and then told him the whole story.

'Uncommonly audacious, I must say !' he answered, more than once ; but when I came to the '*Adesso viene un passaggio*,' he laughed so heartily, that the Prince signed to him to come nearer and explain. However, I begged him to be silent, and feeling that I was safe, so far as he was concerned, I went on my way rejoicing.

At dinner, next day, the Prince summoned me to the table. I knew a storm was brewing, for one of the servants had told me already that I had been the subject of discussion. I came in with a hang-dog look, for the thought that I was to be lectured, not only in the presence of the guests, but of the servants as well, covered me with confusion, so that, in my embarrassment, I got no further than the door.

' Ah !' said the Prince, ' pale as a wench taken before a police-court ! But I'll soon make those cheeks of thine redder ! Who would have thought this fellow would have had the effrontery, only yesterday, to play a sonata in G from one of the parts of a symphony in E *la fa*, and to make a fool of an Ambassador !'

' I had no intention of doing that, Your Highness,' said I, ' for I had made up my mind beforehand, to beg the Ambassador not to betray me to you.'

' Did you really do that ?' said the Prince.

' It was not necessary,' I answered, 'for I soon discovered that he did not know a note.'

' Be that as it may,' continued the Prince, ' it was a bold prank of yours. What do you deserve ?'

I shrugged my shoulders, and stammered out that I ought to be punished.

'Well, come here and get your punishment!'

I expected at least a box on the ear, but instead of that, he gave me his plate, with a glass of Tokay and five or six biscuits on it.

'I promised you to make those white cheeks redder,' said he, as he handed it to me. 'Take it, sit down there, and try whether the colour will not come!'

I did as I was bid, and on taking up the third biscuit, found ten ducats underneath it.

When I wanted to get up and thank him, 'It is because you got out of the scrape so cleverly yesterday!' said the Prince

I think I have said already, that presence of mind was the quality which the Prince liked best to reward, and as it is often found, when you know that it will be noticed, I deserved recognition, on this account, often enough.

About this time, Gluck was summoned to Rome, where he was hailed with enthusiasm, and made a ' Cavaliere dello Sperone d'oro.'

This Order is given in Rome, and the members are entitled ' Comites palatii romani.' They get a diploma, written on parchment, and sealed with a large seal. After their appoint-ment, they enjoy in Rome, as well as in the Papal States, all the privileges of nobility, having the *entrée* of the Pope's palace, besides holding the same rank that chamberlains have at other Courts. Their badge is a Cross of yellow enamel, set in gold, like that of the Knights of Malta, and worn, as they wear it, round the neck, on a scarlet ribbon. Sometimes it is a little smaller and all of gold, and then it hangs by a red ribbon, attached to a button-hole. The Order is of great antiquity, and was formerly much more thought of than at present. With a view of encouraging art and science, the Popes, at a later period, bestowed it upon great and brilliant geniuses, such as Metastasio, Bibiena, Guarini, etc. So it happened that Gluck won this distinction, and always styled himself Cavaliere, Chevalier, or Ritter Gluck.

I ask the reader's indulgence for detaining him so long over the description of this Order, of which I myself became an associate in 1770. But this does not account for my signature, *von* Dittersdorf, for, three years later, I received a patent of nobility from the Imperial Court. You will hear more about this, later on.

CHAPTER XI.

Short exile at Hildburghausen—Schweitzer—The ill-omened sleigh expedition.

THE so-called Seven Years' War broke out in 1758, and in the following year the Prince was appointed to the command of the Imperial army. Fourteen members of his orchestra accompanied him on the campaign, and I and my two brothers were of the number.

In the middle of April, in the same year, the Prince's retinue, with a suitable escort of cavalry, started on its journey, and in the course of a month, we entered Fürth, near Nürnberg, where the Imperial army was to assemble. There we remained for about two months, before the army, consisting of 90,000 men, was got together, and then we marched to Erfurth in Thuringia, where Soubise, the French General, with his 25,000 men, was ready to combine with the Imperial troops. I could tell many a story of this time, if it did not lie outside my plan.

When the two armies advanced, the Prince's suite, baggage and all, protected by an escort of two squadrons of cavalry, was sent back to Hildburghausen. We passed the huge Thuringian forest, and the Sattel,—a high mountain with a road over it. Our line of march was by way of Saalfeld and Jena, with its famous University, and on the tenth day we reached Hildburghausen in safety. This was the residence of the reigning Duke, and we passed the whole of the winter there Every week there was a concert in the Duke's castle, and we always had to appear.

We were on very cordial terms with the Duke's band. One of their number was a youth who, as a boy, had had a lovely soprano voice ; when that changed, he became a cello player among the Duke's musicians. He and I were of the same age, and we were daily in each other's company. My elder brother became so attached to him, that he offered him a home in his own excellent quarters, and, until we left the place, the two friends occupied rooms adjoining one another. This amiable lad was called Schweitzer, and is the same who, later on, became so famous as a composer, especially by his version of Wieland's ' Alcestis.'

I never remember to have passed so delightful

a winter,—and yet I had a hair's-breadth escape, and might have been carried off in the flower of my youth !

One of the Duke's rough-riders, who used to play the violin, had asked me to give him lessons. His father was not too well off; he himself was a very nice fellow. I consented to teach him, but would not take any money ; so his one object was to give me pleasure, and I had no end of carriages and horses. A great fall of snow occurred early in the year, and we had snow throughout the whole winter. Twice every week, he drove me in a sleigh to a very popular inn, half a mile from the town. On one occasion he appeared, dressed in very neat shoes and stockings, and made me put on my Sunday best, as there was to be a grand *fête* that day, in honour of the birthday of a Court advocate, and he was commissioned to give me an invitation to the ball. I might expect one of the Duke's grooms, on a handsome sleigh, to be at my front door at three o'clock. I gladly accepted the invitation, and ransacked my drawers for all my Sunday clothes ; but scarcely had I left my room, when I was seized with panic, and felt as if an icy hand were passing down my back. I am not superstitious, but, somehow or other, all desire for the expedition

vanished.   I shut my cupboard door again, and
sat down to my writing-table, and when the
rough-rider appeared, I told him then and there
that I had changed my mind.   He entreated
me to come, but in vain, though I could assign
no rational excuse for not going.   The barber,
who had just arrived, was dismissed in his
presence.   The rough-rider left, in the sulks,
and made the groom take my place in the
sledge, that it might be properly weighted.
He himself rode on the so-called *Löffel*, and I
watched him from my window, as he drove off,
across the great Square, to the gate of the town.

The sound of the wheels had hardly died
away, when I wrapped myself up in my cloak,
and went to my brother.   I found him with
Schweitzer, poring over Rabener's satires ; they
were reading them out to each other.   We set
to work at the six new quartets by Richter,
which Schweitzer had got hold of.   He played
the cello, I the first violin, my elder brother the
second, and my younger the bass.   In between,
we drank rare good coffee, and smoked the
finest tobacco.   How jolly it was !

We were just tuning for a new quartet, when
a report suddenly reached us, that the rough
rider had had the misfortune to be pitched out
of the sleigh, which had been upset by the

collision of one of the wheels with a stone! The groom's forehead had come into contact with one end of the gate ; his skull was smashed, and he had been killed instantly. Imagine my horror! Schweitzer ran off, to get further information. He returned in half an hour, and confirmed the sad story. They had taken the rough-rider to the Guard-house, where he told Schweitzer that his one comfort in this misfortune was that I had not gone with him, as I should most certainly have been injured in the same way. The Duke bestowed one-half of her husband's wages on the poor widow, for the remainder of her life, and the father of the rough-rider bound himself, by a legal contract, to supply the other half, but the rough-rider himself was put under arrest for four months, for his want of care and caution. Thus I owed my life to a vague presentiment.

We remained here right on into the month of March, when we resumed our rather long and wearisome return journey to Vienna.

CHAPTER XII.

I get into bad company, and take to gambling—Desertion—
Arrest—I am transported to Vienna—My position there.

THE Prince, on resigning his command, was
almost sorry that he had sold Schlosshof, for he
disliked town in summer, preferring a country
life at that season. He determined, therefore, to
take a hunting-lodge, either in Austria or in
Moravia. This resolve kept him constantly on
the move, and we spent many months in idleness.

That was very bad for me. I took up with loose
company, and could not keep out of debt, though
some of my pupils paid handsomely, and added
materially to my income. By playing in churches,
too, and in private houses, I turned many an
honest penny, but it was all no good. By the
middle of the month, every farthing had gone
over billiards, cards, and the skittle-ground. I
succeeded in winning considerable sums at
billiards, now and then, for I was really a good

player. When that happened, I would pay off
my debts and get fresh credit ; however, this
only confirmed me in my loose ways. Not that
my musical studies suffered all this time—music
was still the best part of me. I practised in-
cessantly on the violin, and applied myself
sedulously to composition. I wrote six symphonies, which made a stir both in Vienna and
in Prague.

Count N., a Knight of Bohemia, who had
an orchestra of his own, had got hold of these
symphonies. He came to Vienna, and naturally
wished to make my acquaintance. I was summoned. He ordered me to write six new
symphonies, giving me twenty-four ducats,
twelve of which he paid in advance, while he
commissioned his agent to pay the other twelve,
when I handed over my score. At the same
time, he asked me if I was engaged. I answered
that I was in the Prince's service, at a monthly
salary of thirty-seven florins thirty kreutzers.

'Good heavens !' he cried. 'Those are not
the wages for a man who understands what you
understand ! If you will enter my service, you
shall have sixteen ducats a month, the regula-
tion table, lodgings gratis, and two handsome
suits of clothes every year.

I answered, that it would be ungrateful on

my part, to abandon a Prince through whose liberality I had learnt everything that I knew.

' Do as you please !' replied the Count. ' But should you ever quit your situation, remember that it is always open to you to accept the terms which I offer.'

So I went on from bad to worse, and was always in arrears.   My debts now amounted to some seventy gulden.   If I failed to satisfy my creditors on the first day of the ensuing month, they threatened to complain of me to the Prince. It was hopeless to expect that, with my wages of seven-and-thirty gulden, I could wipe out a debt of sixty gulden, and get my living as well. I told my anxiety to one of my rascally companions, mentioning also the Count's offer, and lo and behold! I let myself be persuaded by him to cut and run.

Next morning, he came to me, with the news that he had already secured a place on the coach which was to start for Prague on the first of the next month.   It wanted but five days to the time, and in that interval I scuttled off to him, carrying clothes, linen, scores, etc. He lent me a small box, in which I packed up my property, and it was duly consigned to the care of the coachman.   I persuaded our paymaster to give me my wages a day earlier than

the first of the month, on which they were due.
My heart often went pit-a-pat, when I thought
upon this base trick ; but matters had gone too
far with me, and I tried, like every double-
dealer, to deafen conscience with the plea of
necessity.

Early on the morning of the appointed day,
I drove away from Vienna, with a troubled
mind. The trees and fields seemed to reproach
me with ingratitude, and, not daring to look at
the beautiful scene, lit up on a bright summer's
morning, I wrapped myself up in my cloak, full
of shame. But my lightheartedness soon got
the better of me, and the farther I went, the
more the movement of the carriage stirred my
blood, the more cheerful and jubilant I became.
Was I not a free man, and master of my own
fate ?

I arrived in Prague, after spending five days
on the road, and hurried off at once to the Count ;
but, good heavens! how I started, when the porter
gave me the sad news that he and the Countess
had gone, three months ago, to Paris, where he
might possibly remain for the next nine months.
I was dumfoundered, and overwhelmed at the
thought of my loneliness. At length I asked
to see the majordomo. I explained to him who
I was, and how the Count had offered me his

services in Vienna.   All I got from him was a
dry answer, to the effect that he had no commission to provide me with money, food, and
lodging.   He had no doubt of the correctness
of my story, but of course he must write to the
Count, and five or six weeks and more must
elapse, before I could get an answer, so I must
be patient.

There was nothing else to be done ; but how
was I to live all that time ?   My small stock of
money would not hold out.   I chanced to have
heard of a fine oboe player, who had been in
the service of Count Breda ; so I looked him up
next morning, and told him of my difficulty,
asking him to get me employment until the
Count's return, though I carefully held back
from him the scandalous story of my leaving
Vienna and deserting the Prince.   The good
man pitied me, and said I should only have a
short time to wait, and he would talk over the
matter with his Count.

He soon returned, and took me off to his
master, who received me very kindly, and told
me not to be anxious.

' My house and table are at your service,'
said he, 'until you get an answer from my good
friend, Count N. ; and if you want to earn
something meanwhile, write me six symphonies

and two concertos for my oboe player. Here is something *a conto*,' and he handed me twelve ducats.

I was saved. Deducting thirty gulden from these ducats, I handed them over to the oboe player, requesting him to forward them to my landlord in Vienna, which he loyally did.

A month passed, and I had finished three symphonies and a concerto for the oboe; the Count gave me twelve ducats more, and I sent off another instalment of forty gulden in the same way.

A day or two afterwards, I was at work on composition, when I was summoned by Count Breda,—and how can I describe my horror, when I saw the face of Bremer, the steward! A policeman stood by his side, and he looked at me gravely and sorrowfully, without saying a word.

'You have landed me in a great difficulty, through your silence about your flight from Vienna,' said the Count angrily. 'There—read for yourself!' and he handed me a legal document, signed by the then Statthalter of Prague, Count Wiepprick, in which Count Breda was strictly ordered to give me up then and there to the police, and to answer the charge of having made me run away from the Prince's service.

' No, no !' I called out. 'Count Breda had nothing whatever to do with my absconding.'

' Is this correct?' asked the commissary.

'As God lives, it is true!' I answered.

My evidence was at once reduced to a protocol, and I made a clean breast of the whole matter. It was read over to me again, and I admitted it and signed it, as did the commissioner.

I promised the Count, as I went with him, to send from Vienna the three symphonies and the oboe concerto, for which he had paid me beforehand ; but he did not accept the offer, and this wounded me more than anything else.

I was obliged to get into a carriage, with the policeman at my side, and was thus conveyed to safe quarters in the Altstädter Rathhaus. My room was very neat ; I had excellent food, but having no sort of appetite for it, I could get nothing down. I was not released from arrest until the third day, and after that I was once more sent back to Vienna, accompanied by Bremer, the commissioner, and two additional policemen.

Once there, I was locked up in a room adjoining the porter's, and shortly afterwards Bremer reappeared ; he, by the Prince's orders, was to try my case over again, and sum it up.

He took down all my answers, which were to the effect that I had run away, partly because I was attracted by the promises of Count N , and partly from fear of my creditors. Everything depended on my clearing myself from the suspicion of having wished to deceive them, and this was not difficult, because they all produced their receipts at once, when I asked for them. This fact altered the state of things very materially, for next morning Bremer returned, and told me, in the Prince's name, that although he entirely acquitted me of dishonourable dealings with my creditors, he must still mete out some punishment for my thankless conduct to himself, my best friend ; his Grace, therefore, ordered me to be kept under arrest in the porter's house for a fortnight, with bread and water every fourth day.

My tears choked me. I could scarcely find words to express my gratitude to so generous a Prince ; but on the evening of the third day, when already I was thinking sorrowfully of the bread and water of the morrow, Bremer took me to him. I felt overwhelmed with penitence and shame, and not daring to look him in the face, I broke out into a violent fit of weeping. The Prince was silent until I checked myself. Then he said :

' I see your own feelings torment you enough. No further punishment is necessary. You are set free from arrest. Perhaps I shall be more likely to help you, if I show mercy, than if I chastise you severelv, as you yourself have owned that you deserve to be chastised. Go ! Live a decent life ı Then I shall forget the shame which you have brought on both of us.'

I went to my room. My constitution was generally good, but this interview had so upset me, that all night long I was hot or cold—in short, I was attacked by a fever, which kept me in bed for a whole month. During my illness I was nursed and tended like one of the family, and the Prince sent to tell me that he had forgiven everything long ago. All I had to do was to keep quiet and get better ! I heard, too, that everyone of the household was forbidden, under pain of dismissal, to reproach me in the smallest degree.

I gradually recovered my health, and for two whole years, whilst I was employed as usual in the Prince's service, I worked hard at music and composition. At last a crisis came, which completely altered my fate.

CHAPTER XIII.

Dismissal of the band—Count Durazzo—My journey to Italy with Gluck — Marini — Sojourn in Venice and Bologna—Farinelli—Nicolini and the blind beggar— A deputation—Father Martin—Panic—Hurried return to Vienna—Lolli and I are rivals.

THE Prince, my patron, was great-uncle of the reigning Duke of Sachsen Hildburghausen, who died about this time,—the hereditary successor to the Dukedom being a child between six and seven years of age. The result was, that not only the guardianship of the ward devolved upon the Prince, but the administration and government of the Duchy as well. He willingly undertook both offices, and moved to Hildburghausen accordingly.

As he found an orchestra ready made at this Court, and as he had his hands full with the education of the hereditary Prince and the administration of the estate, he felt obliged to dismiss the greater part of his own band. To prevent their losing a livelihood, he agreed with Count Durazzo, then the chief director of the Court Theatre, that we should be taken on by him. The contract bound us for three years' service, during which we were obliged to play in the Opera House and at Court, for the same pay that we had received in the Prince's service.

No one suffered more than I did by this arrangement, for I had to play almost daily from 10 a.m. to 2 p.m. at operatic and ballet rehearsals, not to mention theatrical performances from 6.30 to 10.30 of an evening, as well as accompanying at the theatrical concerts, and playing solos every fortnight. I had also bound myself to appear before the Emperor and the Court on *fête* and gala days.

One may easily suppose that, with so much hard work on hand, I had no time for teaching or attending private concerts, so that I was debarred from adding to my income, outside my professional duty. In those days everything was on the most splendid scale, and whenever I had to appear as a *virtuoso* before the public, or even before the Imperial Court, I had to be very careful in the matter of dress. My monthly salary of thirty-seven florins thirty

kreutzers only served to pay for my meals. I
could make no arrangements for dining privately,
for no one, except at the regular hotels, would
have cared to supply me with dinners at two
or perhaps half-past two o'clock. So I had to
pay dearly where I was, and many a day I
squandered a gulden, without getting enough
to eat.

Two years had elapsed since Gluck had been
appointed Kapellmeister, with a salary of two
thousand gulden. He had taken a fancy to
me, when I was with the Prince. I now en-
deavoured to keep myself in his good graces,
and I succeeded so well, that he loved me as his
own son. So I went to him at once, and told
him everything connected with my history; he
promised to interest himself in my behalf.

I accompanied him next day on a visit to
Count Durazzo, and after Gluck had explained
everything, I asked for an increase of pay, or
for leave to resign my office. Gluck, with
much earnestness, supported my request. At
last the Count said to me ·

' My dear boy, I have no power either to
increase your pay, or to accept your resignation,
for I cannot go outside your contract. But
I can dispense with your services for four days
in the week, so that now and then you can

earn something on your own account This
will be a partial relief, anyhow.'

I warmly thanked His Excellency for this
kindness, which served my purpose so well,
that very often my profits exceeded my regular
wages. These I spent on fine clothes, which
so gratified the Count, that he became my
gracious patron, and often invited me to dinner.
In return for his kindness, I redoubled my efforts,
and it was soon my good fortune to secure the
undivided applause of the Viennese public.

Some fifteen months afterwards, Gluck informed me that he was bound for Bologna,
having contracted to write an opera there.
Would I like to travel to Italy with him, of
course on the understanding that I paid one-
half of the travelling expenses, and my own
board? If so, he was quite prepared to get
the consent of Count Durazzo.

'There is *nothing* I should like better,' I
answered, in a state of high enthusiasm, which
such a man as Gluck, who knew of my passion
for art, and was well acquainted with my whole
history, ought to have appreciated. 'But,' I
added sorrowfully, 'I have no means.'

'Oh, indeed!' answered Gluck, turning aside
coldly. 'Then I suppose the plan must fall
through.'

That very same evening, I happened to be
supping with Herr von Preiss, the Hofagent of
the time, and I told him of Gluck's offer.

'Nonsense!' said he 'Strike while the iron
is hot, and take Gluck at his word.'

'All very well,' said I, shrugging my shoulders.
'But where is the money to come from? Gluck
is willing to take me with him, but I am to pay
half the expenses.'

'Pah!' answered the honest fellow—peace be
to his ashes!—'I will see if it cannot be managed.
Here are a hundred ducats for you! You need
not pay me until you are better off. Dine with
me to-morrow! I will invite Herr von Allstern,
and over a good bottle of Grännzinger [the
best Austrian wine] we will try and induce
him to advance you the same amount. Besides
this, in case of emergencies, you shall have my
draft for six hundred gulden, so that altogether
you will be upwards of one thousand five hundred
gulden to the good. That will be enough for
you. We shall not press for payment. See
Gluck as soon as possible to-morrow morning,
square everything, and then come back and
dine with me!'

With tears of joy, I thanked my noble benefactor. Next day I went straight off to Gluck.
The news put him in the highest spirits; he

ordered his carriage, and we drove off to Count
Durazzo, who not only gave me my *exeat*
and presented me with fifty ducats towards my
travelling expenses, but promised me, in addition, a half-yearly advance from the funds of the
theatre.   We prepared to start in a fortnight's
time.

I was highly elated, when I hurried off to
dine with Herr von Preiss, and everything
turned out as he had prophesied on the day
before.   Shortly afterwards, Count Durazzo
invited Gluck and myself to dinner, when
he gave me a draft on the theatre for two
hundred and twenty florins, adding that the
Empress wished to help towards my expenses,
and was prepared to continue my regular salary
during my absence.

'If the funds run short,' he continued, 'Herr
Kapellmeister Gluck will be delighted to advance
money to you, on the assignment of your salary.'

'I shall not need anything,' answered I, quickly
and dryly, 'for two good friends of mine have
provided for every emergency.'

'*Tanto meglio!*' said the Count.

Our journey was postponed for a few days,
on account of a Signora Marini, who had been
engaged as *prima donna* for two whole years
at the theatre at Prague, and now wished to

return with her mother to Venice, her native place. Gluck had known her three years before in Italy, and was good enough to put off the journey for another five days on her account, stipulating, however, that she must consent to travel day and night, without stopping. To this she assented, and we drove away from Vienna in two carriages, with post-horses.

Gluck made me paymaster, and I was to keep the accounts. Signora Marini asked me to do the same thing for her, presenting me with a well-filled purse, which she undertook to replenish when it was empty.

She was a very beautiful and interesting girl of about twenty-four years of age, quick, full of fun, and very amusing. Besides this, her behaviour was dignified and becoming. At our very first dinner in Neustadt, she proposed that we men should change places at every station, as far as Venice, so that she might enjoy the conversation of both. Sometimes Gluck was to ride in her carriage, sometimes myself. Her mother, a bright, cheery lady of some fifty years of age, as outspoken as her daughter, always drove in our carriage, having Gluck for her companion at one time, at another myself,— so it was very pleasant for all of us. Gluck was polite, and wished to make himself agreeable ; but I tried to spoil his game when my turn came, and our little jealousies helped to make the journey more piquant. The maiden was the sovereign Queen, and the Kapellmeister was *Amor*, who set the tune. Gluck's solemn vow to travel day and night was soon undermined, and, in such favourable circumstances, we thought it more comfortable, and more profitable as well, to sleep at Grätz, Laybach, and Görz, than to go jogging on and make nothing except distance.

We arrived at Mestri on the evening of the seventh day of our journey. There we had intended to pass the night, going by water next morning to Venice in a *peota* (a large, two-oared boat, capable of holding from six to ten persons, baggage included) ; but seeing herself so near, and prompted perhaps by the sweet associations of old days, Marini was wilfully bent on persuading us to start that very evening, so we reached the city before twelve o'clock on the night between Palm Sunday and Monday in Holy Week.

Gluck determined to stay a week there. We regretted that our visit happened to come off in Holy Week, when every theatre was shut, and there was no music to be heard,

except an oratorio at the Hospital Agli Incurabili. It is never any good to think too much
of a thing beforehand! Not only had I heard
long ago, in Vienna, that Agli Incurabili and
Alla Pietà possessed a band and chorus, composed of women, which surpassed all other
Italian orchestras and choruses for voices and
execution, but Signora Marini had told me
about it on the journey. Consequently, I was
on the tiptoe of expectation. But what a fraud
it was! The oratorio was a very poor affair ;
the violins were out of tune the whole time,
and when an air was in the key of P *fa* or E *la
fa*, they were an eighth or actually a quarter of
a note too sharp. Their *tempi*, too, seemed to
me all wrong ; sometimes they wobbled, sometimes they dragged, sometimes they hurried.
Barring two singers, one a pure soprano and
the other a full contralto, there was nothing
worthy of the least attention.

By way of compensation for this music, I
saw two *fêtes*, which I thoroughly admired.
One was the evening function on Maunday
Thursday, when Our Lord was carried to the
grave in procession ; the other was the funeral
of the Doge, who had died two days before our
arrival. The great Piazza di San Marco was
illuminated on each occasion—that is to say,

two huge, thick torches blazed in front of every window of the palaces on all sides of it. The effect was magnificent. There were solemn processions around this solid and splendid square ; it was hard to say which was the more imposing ceremony—the burial of Our Lord, or that of the Doge.

We started for Bologna on Easter Eve. The opening of the grand new opera-house built entirely of freestone, was fixed for Whit Monday. The old theatre had been burnt to the ground a year before, and the new building was raised by the subscriptions of the wealthiest and foremost people of the city. The manager, Count Bevilaqua, an associate of the company, had selected Metastasio's opera, ' Il Trionfo di Clelia,' as the opening piece, and Gluck was engaged to write the music for it. Mansoli, the famous *castrato*, was *primo uomo ;* the *prima donna* was Signora Girelli Aquilar, whose husband, a Spaniard by birth, was a famous oboist, in no way inferior to the world-renowned Besozzi. A young *castrato*, Toschi by name, was *secondo uomo*. Two years afterwards, he was engaged at Vienna. I have forgotten the name of the *seconda donna*, a pretty girl of seventeen, with a clear and agreeable voice, though she was only a beginner.

The *primo tenore* was the famous Giuseppe
Tibaldi, whom Gluck afterwards engaged for
Vienna, where he greatly distinguished himself.
At the head of the first violins was Luchini
of Milan, in those days an orchestral player
of mark. At the head of the seconds was
Spagnoletti, who was equally famous. He had
been imported from Cremona. The band consisted of about seventy persons. With Italian
orchestras of that size, two pianos are required
and Mazzoni, the well-known Kapellmeister,
presided at the second. He had settled in
Bologna, and was the paid Kapellmeister of
many of the leading churches, convents, and
bishops' palaces.

Count Bevilaqua, a courteous man, received
us very kindly. Gluck introduced me to him
as his pupil, for we had agreed that I was not
to give myself out as a soloist till we had
heard all the best violinists.

Gluck told the Count of his wish to hear
the opera-singers, so he forthwith arranged for
a concert, to be given by thirty of the best
artists, on the following afternoon, at his house,
we three being the only persons present. I
was enchanted with Girelli, Mansoli, and Tibaldi,
but what took me most of all, was an air in
which Aquilar accompanied his wife on the

oboe.   Luchini and Spagnoletti each played
a violin concerto.   Gluck whispered to me ·

'You have nothing to fear from these two
magicians!'

I thought as he did, but I said :

'I think they are both very good, only
everyone has a different method.'

Gluck only began to compose now, but as he
had already got well ahead with his work in
Vienna, the first act was ready for the copyist
in ten days' time.   He worked of a morning
and evening, never of an afternoon.   After
dinner, we used to pay visits, and then we
went to the coffee-house, where we generally
stayed until supper-time.

One of our first visits was to the great
Farinelli, who, as my readers already know,
had come to Vienna, after the death of his
illustrious benefactor, the King of Spain.   He
was at that time an old man of nearly eighty
years of age.   Now and then he asked us
to dinner, and treated us royally, which was
not surprising, for he was almost a millionaire.
I reminded him of Madame Tesi, and told
him that I had lived in the same house with
her for years; of course that made him take
an interest in me.

Another of our visits was to Padre Martino,

the world-renowned dictator of classical music. He was nearly as old as Farinelli, and they were bosom friends. Gluck, too, had known him for years, and never passed through Bologna without paying his respects to the '*Padre di tutti i Maestri*,' as all Kapellmeisters call him to this day.

The Kapellmeister, Mazzoni, chanced to hear that I was a violin-player. When he had heard me, he begged me to play at the great Church festival, which was to be held in San Paolo, for which he had composed two sets of Vespers, as well as a Mass. Would I play a solo for him, at the early service to-morrow?

I consented.

On the afternoon of the day before the great *fête*, Gluck and I went to the church, to hear Mazzoni's first set of Vespers. Chorus and band consisted of over a hundred. Though it was a fine, majestic work, I thought it too lively and secular for the church. Barring the masterly fugues, it was more like an *opera seria* than sacred music. Between the Psalms, Spagnolétti played a concerto by Tartini, which I had practised some years before. The church was crowded with connoisseurs and amateurs. You could see, from the faces of the audience, that he had made his mark.

'You may safely reckon on the applause of your audience to-morrow,' said Gluck to me, 'for your music, like your playing, is much more modern.'

It had already got wind that a German *virtuoso* was going to play a solo on the violin, at High Mass next day. As we left the church, we overheard two gentlemen talking together.

'To-morrow morning we are to hear a German *virtuoso*,' said one; to which the other answered

'I am afraid he will make a fool of himself, now we have heard that excellent Spagnoletti.'

But next day, when I played a concerto of my own composition, the gentleman turned out to be a false prophet, for Gluck, Herr Bevilaqua, and Signor Mansoli congratulated me on my complete conquest of the audience. Gluck told me that he had elbowed his way to our two critics of yesterday, so as to hear their opinion. One of them exclaimed:

'*Per Dio!* that lad plays like an angel!'

And the other had chimed in:

'How is it possible that a German tortoise should arrive at such perfection?'

Whereupon he had taken the liberty to say to the second:

'By your leave, sir, I too am a German tortoise, and in spite of that, I have the honour of writing the new opera for the opening of the theatre which has just been restored.'

At this, one of them caved in, declaring that he was entirely cured of his early prejudice against the German nation.

Gluck had hardly finished his story, when the Father Prior of the convent arrived, accompanied by two additional chaplains. He thanked me for the trouble I had taken, and, ' Having seen from my confessional how you pleased the congregation,' said he, ' may I ask you to play another concerto at Vespers this evening ?'

I absolutely declined to do so, but the good Prior persisted in his entreaties, and on Count Bevilaqua's assuring me that, ever since Bologna became a city, no *virtuoso* had been similarly honoured, and that I should create a universal sensation, I consented.

In the evening the church was crowded ; hundreds were sent away, there was no room for them ; but if I had played well in the forenoon, I played twice as well then.

After Vespers, we were entertained in the convent—Gluck, I, Mazzoni, and the two *castrati*, Potenza and Nicolini, who had sung in the service, were the guests. The supper was really of the Sardanapalus order, for every dainty to be found in Italy at that season was on the table. We caroused up to nearly midnight, and then went home, shouting in chorus.

I must really tell a little story about this man Nicolini,—I saw and heard all that passed, myself. Like many of the young *castrati*, he was a lively, go-ahead fellow, a bumptious talker, and a bit of a coxcomb. He was too much addicted to star-gazing to mind where he was going. We were cutting off a corner, to get into another street, when he stumbled over a blind beggar sitting upon the ground, whom he had not noticed, and so came to grief. Bursting with rage, he shrieked out, in his shrill soprano voice :

'Eh, you d——d blind dog!'

The beggar, taking the soprano voice for a woman's, gave him a Roland for an Oliver.

'Eh, you street-poll!' cried he. 'You're a pretty sort, to be abusing a poor blind beggar!'

We all burst out laughing, though we had our misgivings about the way Nicolini would treat the wretched creature. He felt in his pockets, however, and taking out two lire, placed them in the beggar's hand, observing :

'Well, old boy, for once in your life you have made a good guess, so here are a couple of lire for you!'

The blind man, full of gratitude when he actually felt the coins in his palm, clasped his hands over his crutch, and said ·

'May the Lord requite you, and give you grace to be penitent like the Holy Magdalen, so that you may give up your shameful life, and do penance for it!'

We had had a good laugh before, but now we fairly exploded; it was one of the funniest scenes I ever saw.

The story soon went the whole round of Bologna, and from that hour Nicolini was dubbed '*la Santa Magdalena.*'

It is the custom in Italian monasteries, when they honour anyone with a gift, to carry it in public procession to his room. The leader is usually dressed in a black Spanish cloak, and wears a great wig; he is followed by two acolytes, dressed in surplices, who carry the present upon a huge two-handled silver salver, covered with a piece of damask. Behind them come two lay brothers in their monks' dress, over which they wear white rochets. The fortunate man may be living quite close to the cloister, but—good heavens! the vanity of these monks!—this caravan is bound to go winding about through the principal squares and streets of the town all the same, and although everyone knows what is going on perfectly well, yet the leader of the procession is commanded to explain to every inquirer whence the present comes, whither it is going, and why it is given.

My host came to me, next morning, to tell me that a deputation from San Paolo was at the door, asking to see me. I was going to have a present, he said, and I should have to give the man who brought it a scudo to drink my health. I admitted the deputation. The foreman addressed me in a speech which lasted over a quarter of an hour. This was nothing else than messages of thanks from the Prior and all the convent, coupled with an earnest prayer that, in consideration of their abundant poverty, I would deign to accept their little present. Remembering yesterday's Sardanapalian feast, I felt sceptical as to the poverty. The present consisted of over twenty pounds' weight of magnificent candied fruits, with all sorts of choice confectionery   That was not all! There were six pairs of white silk and six pairs of black silk Naples stockings, six double-silk Milanese pocket-handkerchiefs, and twelve larger and smaller relics, which were all set in silver filigree. I sent my thanks to the Prior and all the convent, and gave Demosthenes in a wig his scudo.

After many bowings and scrapings, the deputation withdrew.

We were just setting out for the coffee-house, on the afternoon of that very day, when the Padre Martino paid us his return visit. He seized the opportunity of asking me to play a concerto in his church, at a great function which was impending. Of course I was to be paid for it—would I be content with the ordinary fee of twelve double ducats? I said I would only play on condition that I was not paid. What I prized, beyond money, was the honour of being selected to play by 'the Father of Music.' The good old man thanked me for my 'pretty way of thinking of him,' as he called it, and after another half-hour's conversation, he went away as he came, leaning on the arm of a lay brother, and supported by a stick.

It was soon the talk of all Bologna, that I had been invited by Padre Martino to assist at the grand ceremony, on the first day of the festival *'per la visità della Madonna di San Lucca,'* and everyone knew that I had refused to be paid, and had promised my services solely for the honour of God.

The day approached for the opening of the festival, which was to be inaugurated by the procession of the miracle-working portrait of

the Madonna, said to have been painted by
St. Luke. The *fête* lasted for three days. We
went to church to hear Vespers,—the music by
Padre Martino. What a gulf between that and
Mazzoni's work! I have never heard sacred
music so majestic, so lofty, and so touching!
Even Caldara's composition is far inferior to it.
In one Psalm—I think a 'Magnificat'—the
'Amen' was an eight-part fugue, a marvel of
artistic elaboration. The effect made by that
glorious fugue may be imagined, for the band
consisted of one hundred and sixty people, and
the chorus was eighty strong.

On the following morning, Gluck and I called
on the venerable musician, who had asked us
to drink chocolate with him. We were full
of admiration for his fine music, *i.e.*, the Vespers
which we had heard.

'I think it probable,' said he, 'that yesterday's
Vespers and to-day's High Mass will be my
Swan Song, for I am conscious already that
my powers, physical and mental, are beginning
to fail.'

We expressed our regret that we might,
perhaps, never have another opportunity of
hearing the eight-part fugue.

'I'll set that right,' answered the kindly old
man. 'I will make the fugue do duty for

the " Amen " in the " Credo "; they are both in the same key, and so far your wishes shall be gratified.'

I did my very best with my concerto, which I played very successfully in the 'Graduale,' for I had carefully prepared myself for it a week before. Soon after I had finished my concerto, I went with Gluck into the body of the church, to hear the 'Credo' and the 'Amen' at a distance. That day, we discovered all sorts of beauties in the eight-part fugue, which had escaped us the day before. We returned home in a high state of exaltation, and sat down to dinner. Afterwards, our landlord came in, bringing with him a good-sized paper parcel with a seal on it, and said :

' Padre Martino sends you both a few pounds of chocolate.'

He had written on the packet with a very shaky pen : ' 12 *libre per il mio caro amico, il Cavagliere Gluck, e* 12 *libre per il mio caro figliuolo, il Signor Carlo Ditters.'*

Next morning, our landlord informed us that a lad was outside the door, asking to see me, but he seemed to be such a ragged scarecrow, that he had thought twice about letting him in. The beggar, however, would not be put off.

' I advise you not to remain alone with him,'

he added. 'It is hardly safe. However, I will bring up my two stout menservants ; then he may come. Meantime, bolt the door behind me at once, and do not open it again till you hear me calling.'

My landlord went away. I unlocked the door, and asked Gluck to come up to my room. To make things doubly sure, I took both my pocket-pistols ; one I hid under my dressing-gown, and Gluck hid the other in the same way.

After a short interval, I heard a knock at the door, and our landlord introduced himself, with the words : '*È permesso ?*'

I unfastened the bolt. Gluck and I were standing behind a table, in the middle of the room. The first to enter was my landlord ; the servants remained at the door. The ragged gentleman was behind them, and he asked me whether I was the young German *virtuoso* who had played yesterday at the Minorites.

'Yes. And what more do you want ?' said I, playfully drawing out the pistol from under my dressing-gown, Gluck following suit.

He grinned, and, looking at the two servants, said in an off-hand way :

'You might have spared yourself all this fuss. Spite of my rags and tatters, I am a *galant' uomo.*'

' That may be,' said the landlord ; ' but what do you want ?'

He made no reply, but dived into his jacket, and drew out a letter and a small box, both of which he placed on the table.

' What is that ?' said I.

' I do not know. Have the goodness to read the note !'

I read as follows (it was written in Italian. in a carefully-disguised hand) ·

' Please accept the small box, herein enclosed, as a proof of the pleasure with which I heard you yesterday, in the church of the Minorites. I will thank you to sign the enclosed receipt.'

I asked the messenger to open the little box. It contained a handsome gold watch. I signed the receipt, and the bearer took it away, pushing back the scudo which I offered him. Neither prayers nor threats would induce him to tell the name of the donor.

' I gave my word not to betray him,' he said. ' *Son galant' uomo, e tanto basta.*'

And so he left.

We kept on trying to guess who could have sent the present, and at last we set it down to the Minorite Fathers.

Next day we were dining with Farinelli, to

meet a distinguished party. I started, when I saw that his butler had the same features as the mysterious stranger of yesterday. After dinner, I asked him a few commonplace questions. The tone of his voice was exactly the same,— so I knew where I was. Farinelli protested in vain ; he was obliged to confess, but would not hear of gratitude—not a word more was to pass on the subject !

At last we heard Gluck's opera, which was a great success, though the performance fell far short of the composer's ideal. We had been told all sorts of things about Italian orchestras, but Gluck was not in the least satisfied with them. There had been seventeen full rehearsals ; and in spite of that, we missed the *ensemble* and the precision to which we had been accustomed in Vienna.

After the third *Recita* we wanted to go back to Venice, in order to hear the new operas there. Four or five theatres are always open in Venice, during Ascensiontide. Then we had hoped to visit Milan, Florence, and the other famous towns and cities of Italy, but letters reached us from Count Durazzo, calling us back to Vienna, as the coronation of Joseph II. (afterwards Emperor), as King of the Romans, was to take place at Frankfort-on-the-Maine early

in the autumn. This made us alter our plans.
Meanwhile, we started on another short expedition to Parma, where we heard 'Catone in
Utica,' an opera by 'the London Bach,' as he
is called in Germany. Some of the airs were
quite beautiful, but the main body of the work
was written very sketchily, after the Italian
style. At Parma we determined to vary our
journey to Vienna, and go by way of Mantua,
Klagenfurth, and Trent, and we had only just
returned, when we were told that the coronation
had been postponed for another year. It was
very trying to have had to come away from
Italy so soon, for no earthly good.

Whilst I was in Italy, Lolli, the great
violinist, had come to Vienna, where he stayed
some months, and reaped a rich harvest. On
the very evening of my arrival, my elder
brother could not say enough about the sensation caused everywhere by his playing. I
asked about his style, and he gave me one of
his sonatas, of which he had got possession,
and told me I could find out his method from
that, for he repeated himself, with a few variations, in all his pieces. I looked it through,
and quite understood what he meant, when I
saw what very strange passages there were.

'How about his adagio?' I asked.

'Nothing out of the way,' my brother said. 'It is full of twirligigs and jumps. Your friends, however, are very sorry for you, for it is the common cry in Vienna, "Well, our poor Ditters is completely cut out!" But I know for a certainty that, after a week's work, you will be able to imitate all those passages.'

'God forbid!' said I. 'I must do just the reverse, and try to make a better figure in the adagio by good solid playing and expression.'

Next day, I went with Gluck to Count Durazzo, to announce our return. I asked him to dispense with my solo playing for one month, because, whilst I was away from Vienna, I had sketched out some new concertos, and I should have to finish them up, and learn them thoroughly, before I could exhibit my new ideas in public.

'Bravo, my son!' said the Count. 'You shall have six weeks, for you have a difficult task before you. Lolli has made a great hit, no doubt, but I will stake my faith on you!'

I locked myself into my study, shammed an illness, and worked from morning to night. Before another month was out, I went to the Count, and said I was quite ready. So he fixed my *début* for the next concert-day at the theatre.

I played my new concerto, the opening allegro of which contained no very formidable difficulties. I took pains to give the adagio, which followed, in the style I had often heard adopted by Potenza, the famous *castrato* at Bologna, and I made a great point of copying his *Rubbamento di Tempo*. But in order to show my hearers that I was up to difficulties, I had sufficiently peppered the finale with passages which looked very difficult, but which lay well to the hand. The audience was so surprised, that they applauded to a man, shouting :

'*Finale da capo !   Finale da capo !*'

Stimulated by these cheers, I repeated the movement, which I took at a still quicker pace, playing it with the greatest ease. In the final cadenza I fell into a cappriccio, passed through arpeggios into different keys, and after extricating myself, ended with a double shake, which I had never used in public before. In short, I had the good luck to unhorse Lolli, and there was a general cry throughout Vienna :

'Lolli is a tip-top fellow—so is Ditters, but Ditters goes to the heart !'

During the rest of the summer and the following winter, when I was off duty, I often came into contact with the amiable Joseph Haydn. What lover of music does not know the name and the

beautiful works of this distinguished writer?
When we heard any new music by other composers, we criticised it between ourselves,
praising, or the reverse, as we thought just.

I advise every young artist to found an
alliance, at starting, with one of his colleagues,—
stipulating that jealousies and envy are out of
the reckoning.   Haydn and I did this in a spirit
of inquiry, and if all prejudices are laid aside, I
maintain that nothing so materially assists a
young musician's progress as mutual and
friendly criticism of this kind.   It has this
further advantage, that, besides enabling a
writer to introduce many a fine effect with
certainty, it will teach him carefully to avoid
those rocks against which this or that other
composer has come to grief.   I am not saying
anything new.   All the world knows that
criticism—the honest, impartial criticism of
real judges—has ever been of the greatest
use to the fine arts.

CHAPTER XIV.

Poor wages for my attendance at the coronation of Joseph II.
—Count Spork and I at loggerheads—The Bishop of
Grosswardein—My engagement.

THE time for the coronation of the Archduke
Joseph was drawing near. Count Durazzo, who
had accompanied us to Frankfort, summoned
Gluck, Quadagni the *castrato*, myself, and twenty
other persons of the orchestra of the Imperial
Court, to attend the grand ceremony. The two
first received six hundred gulden for travelling
expenses, besides six gulden for daily maintenance. I, and the other twenty, had only half
this allowance. When numbers of people
congregate together, provisions, of course, are
dearer, and you may well believe that, what
with this, and what with our journey, our
finances were at a low ebb. There was no
question of laying by ; instead of earning anything, we had to contribute.

9

My passport described me as a *virtuoso* of the Imperial Court, and in that capacity I made my first appearance in Frankfort at the Römer, and my second at the Imperial quarters, each time on the occasion of a public dinner, when I played a concerto. It was my ambition to do honour to the Emperor, so I bought two handsome suits of clothes, which cost me some seven hundred gulden, in the hope that I should receive a substantial *douceur*, which I was assured officially would be forthcoming. But it often happens in this world that the most deserving is the worst off, and so it turned out in my case. When we got back to Vienna, Gluck and Quadagni received three hundred ducats each, besides their expenses, and I, poor devil! not more than fifty. So it is obvious, that the honour of having figured as titular *virtuoso* at the greatest function of Germany damaged me to the extent of over four hundred ducats. Even Count Durazzo was angry when he heard of it, but, having plenty of money, he gave me fifty ducats out of his own purse.

My contract was to come to an end in a few months' time, so we stipulated that I was to have a yearly salary of one thousand gulden. In return for this I was to play solos, as I did formerly, in the theatre and at Court, besides acting as first violin at the Italian Opera. Three days later the Count announced to me that he had been appointed Imperial Ambassador at Venice, but that, so soon as Count Wenzel Spork had arrived from Prague, he would strongly recommend me to him, and try and induce him to continue the contract which had been made by word of mouth.

Count Spork arrived a fortnight later, and took up the direction of affairs. I called and was admitted. When I entered, he was lying stretched on the sofa, and he made no attempt to rise. He began thus :

' I know that his contract with the theatre will soon be at an end. He must listen to what I have to say. Is he willing to re-engage at the same salary as before ?'

The *he* roused my wrath.

' Will Your Excellency pardon me,' I answered. ' What have I done that I should be addressed in this manner ? I have often had the honour of dining with Your Excellency's predecessor and other Imperial Geheimraths, and none of them ever called me *he*. I am unused to such humiliation ; it offends me.'

The Count started, and stroked his chin with an embarrassed air, saying in a confused tone :

'Really? Mighty fine people, you young fellows! However, it's no matter to me; so, are *you* willing to make a fresh agreement?'

I said that I could serve no longer for such paltry pay. He was prepared to increase it, but he never rose to anything like those thousand gulden. I told all that had passed to Count Durazzo.

'Wait till he has heard you play, then he will come round to your terms!' said he. 'If he does not, then follow me to Venice, and I will give you two hundred ducats, lodgings, and board.'

But I knew that neither the Ambassadors themselves, nor the people of their suite, would be allowed to associate with native Venetians— it is opposed to their State policy—so I very courteously declined to negotiate.

I will now tell of the scheme which I planned, with the view of making myself necessary to Count Spork, as well as to the Viennese public. Having ascertained beforehand that it would be my turn to play a solo in the theatre on the following Friday, I determined to pretend I was ill, and unable to play for a month at least, that I might gain time to finish and to learn some concertos which I had already begun. As I ran the risk of being found out, however, I determined to have another dislocation of the shoulder. I could rely on the loyalty of my servant, and on the silence of my barber; so I stayed at home, and whenever anyone called, I sprinkled the room with spirits of camphor, and pushed a pillow under my dressing-gown, just over my right shoulder. Nobody doubted the truth of my misfortune.

Within three weeks, everything was in readiness. My voluntary imprisonment was telling upon me, and I began to long to get out again. My first visit was to Count Spork. I easily induced him to believe that I could not play under a fortnight's time, — and he gave his consent gladly enough.

At last the evening came on which I was to appear. The theatre was crammed full. My new concerto was such a success that I had to repeat the last allegro, taking it at a quicker pace, and introducing variations, which were greatly applauded.

The Count summoned me next morning.

' I see I must increase your salary,' said he.

He offered seven hundred ; he offered eight hundred gulden. I refused.

' Well,' said he, ' that is as much as I can do.'

' As Your Excellency pleases,' I replied, made my bow, and left the room.

About this time the Bishop of Grosswardein

arrived in Vienna. He was a member of the illustrious Croatian family of Patachich, and had been summoned to the Diet at Pressburg, like most of the other Hungarian magnates. He had heard me play at Court, and now he told me of his passionate love of music; adding that he had a band and chorus of his own, and that Michael Haydn (Joseph's brother, who had hitherto acted as conductor), was going to Salzburg as Concertmeister. Would I take his post, at an annual salary of twelve hundred gulden, board, lodging, maintenance included, with livery and maintenance for my servant? I told him that I should not hesitate to close with the offer, but for the fact that I was actually in negotiation with the directors of the theatre, assuring him at the same time that, if this arrangement fell through, I was at his service. I learnt from him that he meant to stay at Vienna three days longer, at the end of which time he must know definitely what I intended to do, so I promised to give him a formal answer within that time.

On the third day I went to Count Spork, and after a long talk, he agreed to raise my salary to nine hundred florins.

I was not satisfied.

'I am sorry to be forced to leave my native place for such a trifle,' said I at last.

'Come,' he replied; 'I will be reasonable, and to prevent you from saying that I drove you out, you shall have another fifty florins.'

Then I blurted out peevishly:

'If Your Excellency gave me nine hundred and ninety-nine florins, fifty-nine kreutzers, and the sixtieth kreutzer were wanting, I should decline.'

He (very angrily): 'Hoity-toity! this young fellow has many of the tricks of a *virtuoso*, and, over and above that, a pretty good show of the *virtuoso's* impertinence!'

I (coldly): 'Will Your Excellency please to speak out at once? There must be no mistake, for I must know to-day how I stand.'

He: 'This very day?'

I: 'Yes, Your Excellency.'

He (in a passion): 'This very day does not suit me. Be off with you, and do not come to me again till I send for you!'

I bowed and left, going straight off to the inn where the Bishop of Grosswardein was staying. I came to an agreement with him, and promised to appear at Pressburg, bag and baggage, the beginning of the following month,—whereupon he at once advanced me a hundred ducats.

I played my second new concerto that same

evening, just as effectively as before, and Count Spork beckoned to me from his box to come to him.

' I certainly was much hurt by your defiant answer,' said he, ' but I will overlook that, and agree to give you the thousand gulden which you asked for.'

I told him how I was circumstanced, and, however sorry he might be, at least he saw at once that I had not meant to wound him by my passionate demand ; he had the kindness to ask me to dine with him on the following day.

When dinner was over, he took me aside, and said :

'If Hungary does not suit you, you can always depend upon taking up your salary of a thousand gulden here again.   Meantime, as you have shown some talent for ballet writing in the *Pas des deux* which you composed for the Turchi and Paganina, you shall write four such ballets every year, and this will increase your pay by another hundred ducats.   I am very sorry to be forced to lose you, but my hands are tied at Court, and I have to adapt myself to circumstances.   For the same reason, I have been forced to dismiss every member of the Hildburghausen orchestra who demanded an increase of salary, or leave to quit the service.'

I was astonished to hear the Count address me so kindly and confidentially, when he had been so brusque with me before.

'If I have offended you by my bold answers, Your Excellency will forgive me,' said I. 'I did not then know the real kindness of your heart.

He pressed my hand, and answered, with a smile ·

'And I did not know your value as an artist, and the firmness of your character,—so we had best forget what has passed. You will always find a friend in me.'

Who would have dreamt that we should part so amicably ?

CHAPTER XV.

Arrival at *Pressburg*—Journey to *Prague*—*Pichel.*

I ARRIVED safely in Pressburg at the time agreed on. During our first conversation, the Bishop said to me :

' Now that I have got you, I am more eager than ever to indulge my favourite hobby, so far as I can ; and with an income of eighty thousand florins, why should I not ? So I have made up my mind to spend sixteen thousand florins a year on my band and chorus. Here is a list of all the present members, and here is another of those whom I wish to have ! I give you a commission to go to Vienna and to Prague on this business, at my expense, and my steward shall accompany you, to assist in settling the contracts.'

At Prague I addressed myself to Herr Strohbach, first violin at the Italian Opera, and asked for his advice. He said that he would send me a young man whom he could recommend as a good orchestral player, and he thought that his large acquaintance might be of use to me.

Next morning, a young man of the name of Pichel arrived. I found him most attractive. He not only offered me his services in the orchestra, but gave me an opportunity of hearing the other musicians, who might suit my purpose, at a *Collegium Musicum* in the Carmelite Church. Besides Pichel and Fuchs, who played their violin concertos admirably, I heard a man of the name of Ungericht, a good hand in the orchestra, and a bass singer as well; also Herr Satza, a first-rate German flute-player; and Oliva and Pauer, two good wind-instrument players. I engaged all of these.

The first time I heard them play a symphony, I was so satisfied with the excellence of the orchestra that I quietly sent off a messenger to fetch my violin and my music. When everyone had had his turn, I said:

'Gentlemen, you have played for me, it is only fair that I should return the compliment!'

I gave a new symphony of my own, conducted it myself, and wound up with a concerto and a sonata, whereupon Pichel persuaded me to appear in public, kindly undertaking to make all the necessary arrangements during my short stay in the place. He fixed the day of the concert, and as everyone played gratuitously, I netted four hundred and eighteen florins, twenty-eight of which I spent on a supper to the band.

When I was in Vienna, I engaged as cellist Wenzel Himmelbauer, who afterwards became very popular. My double-bass was the worthy Pichelberger. Circumstances prevented me from making terms with the famous clavi-cembalist and organist, Father Michael of the Minorites ; that could only be done by the immediate intervention of the Bishop with the Head of the Order. My recruits met at the time appointed, and the Bishop, who approved my choice, cheerfully acceded to the terms which I had made.

Whilst I was occupied with my commission business, the Bishop engaged a first-rate tenor, —Herr Renner, a pupil of Bonno's ; but we went to Grosswardein at the beginning of April, and he did not come until August.

So now everything was arranged as far as possible.

CHAPTER XVI.

I become a conductor — My first efforts — Renner — Ungericht — Father Michael, Stadler, etc. — My first
grand cantata — A new theatre built — My oratorio,
'Isacco' — Short adventure with the daughter of a
noble *Cassæ perceptor*.

ON our arrival, the Bishop summoned a meeting
of the local musicians of Grosswardein, as well
as the new-comers. These, including the members of the cathedral choir, met in the great
dining-hall, where I was formally introduced to
them as their new conductor. At the same
time the Bishop gave orders that I should be
strictly obeyed, and I was entrusted with full
power to dismiss from service, at my own
option, any renegade from duty, or anyone
who made himself obnoxious, without asking
too many questions.

' I authorize my conductor to settle every
dispute amongst yourselves,' he added, ' and I

expect that his judgment will be as much respected as if it were my own. Should anyone wish me to interfere as arbitrator, his petition must come to me through the conductor, who will report my decision afterwards.'

There is no doubt that this arrangement put very extensive power in the hands of the conductor, under certain circumstances. It might have been much abused, and the rights of the orchestra infringed upon, though, on the other hand, it was very necessary for the preservation of order; for musicians are often quick-tempered, fussy, and troublesome, and too apt to pick a quarrel with their commanders.

When the Bishop had left, I made my speech :

' Gentlemen, though, with the exception of Herr Pichel, I am the youngest man among you, you need not fear that I shall abuse my authority. I have served for a period of twelve years at a still greater Court than this, and have learnt well enough the art of obeying a master. Let me beg of you to bear and forbear with each other ! No one at Court is more subject to the envy and dislike of other servants, whether of higher or lower rank, than a member of the orchestra, because a musician is looked upon as an idle fellow, who does not deserve his pay. They do not understand the amount of trouble and time it costs to make a musician who can earn an honourable livelihood. So let us hold together, and show the world what mutual respect means! I promise you, on my honour, that if any one of you meets with the smallest undeserved insult, even from one of the State officials, I will never rest until the fullest satisfaction is given by the wrong-doer. Lastly, I beg of you only to treat me as your superior when I am *à la tête* of the orchestra, and I assure you that, off parade, you may consider me as your most intimate friend and brother.'

They all assured me that they would get on well together, and would obey me as if they were one man. They kept their word most loyally.

The Bishop allowed me a week's interval before the first full performance. During that time I ordered long desks and benches to be made, for I introduced the Viennese plan of using these for the orchestra, which was so arranged that every player fronted his audience. The concerts were on Sundays and Tuesdays. Everyone connected with the Cathedral, besides the Imperial officers and the nobility of Grosswardein, had a free entry, and could attend the Bishop's reception afterwards.

The orchestra consisted of thirty-four persons.

Amongst them were nine servants in livery, a valet, and a confectioner, besides seven musicians, members of the Chapter, who received extra pay from the Bishop, so that five thousand gulden still remained in the treasury for all that was wanted.

The Bishop attended the first rehearsal. We had played through my new symphony with trumpets and drums, when I stood up and addressed the band:

'Gentlemen, let me remind you—though I speak solely to the less experienced hands—that many wrong notes have been played! I cannot overlook this. First of all, some of us were not in tune at starting; secondly, the marks of expression were not correct; thirdly, some hurried, others dragged the *tempi*, and lastly—and this I cannot forgive—the rests were all wrong. When we go through the work again, let me hope that everyone will note his own blunders and do better. But if my present warning is unheeded, and I have to call anyone to order in public, it will be his fault, not mine. Now tune, everyone together, and then—*da capo !*'

The symphony was repeated, this time all right.

'Bravo!' I cried. 'That's the only way, if

you and I are to be a credit to one another, and all of us to His Excellency, our gracious master. And now, *basta* for to-day!"

The band dispersed, but the Bishop beckoned to me to follow him into his room.

'Thanks for the resolute speech you made to my men!' he said. 'I daily congratulate myself on having engaged you. You shall have a slight proof of my gratification at once.'

He sent off there and then for the receipt which I had given him for the hundred ducats lent to me in Vienna, and tore it up. I kissed his hand, and said ·

'Your Excellency is too good to me to-day, but dare I solicit one more favour?'

The Bishop looked rather startled, but at length he asked what I wanted.

'I want Your Excellency to call me *Du* instead of *Sie*,' I said. 'My old master, the Prince of Hildburghausen, who was like my second father, accustomed me to it; and you, too, are so fatherly, that I cannot but ask for this favour.'

'Be it so!' said the Bishop, after a pause; 'if you are bent upon it. And, as you wish to take me for your father, I must treat you, if you please, as my son.'

Then he brushed away the rising tears.

10

Kind gentleman! he was tenderness itself, and would weep for joy, if it was in his power to make anyone happy; but what made him weep most was music, pathetically played. Nor could anybody accuse him of unmanliness, for he was so earnest and strenuous in action that his conduct, at times, seemed to be hard, and I observed this in many instances.

Our excellent tenor, Renner, arrived at last, his wife and children with him. His fine delivery, choice Italian, beautiful clear voice, and finished vocalization placed him in the foremost rank of singers. He had a large compass, and a gift of using the falsetto so skilfully and easily that it seemed like his natural voice.

Besides Renner and Ungericht, we had also two *castrati*, a soprano, and a contralto. One was a good cellist, the other a good violin-player, so the Bishop increased the pay that they had from the Cathedral, giving them board and lodging in addition.

We had twelve solo-players and four singers in our orchestra. Fuchs, Pichel, and I repre-sented the violins, Father Michael the piano, Pohl and Stadler the oboe, Fournier the clarionet, Satza the flute, Himmelbauer the cello, Pichel-berger the double-bass, Oliva and Pauer the horns. I had arranged that everyone, if summoned to any extra duty, should be ready to take it up at once.

As early as September, I began to think about the Bishop's Name-day, which fell late in December. After conferring with Pichel, who was not only a good Latin scholar, but had a vein of real poetry in him, and could write good Latin verse, we determined to have a complimentary Ode for four voices and chorus. I was obliged to choose Latin, because no one understood Italian except the Bishop, two of the Canons, and myself, whereas every gentleman in Grosswardein, and some of the ladies too, knew Latin. Pichel set to work, and when he had finished his libretto, I showed it to the Bishop, and told him of my intention. It was agreed that this cantata, which, we could see beforehand, would last fully two hours, should be given the evening before, instead of the usual concert. The Bishop himself undertook that the orchestral platform should be raised for the occasion, railed in, and properly decorated. He carried out the plan very well.

I took five weeks over my work, but I foresaw that more chamber music would be wanted on the evening of the *fête*-day. Accordingly, whilst the copyist was transcribing the Latin cantata, I wrote two grand new symphonies for the beginning and end of the performance, besides a symphony with obbligato wind-instruments to come between, and also a new violin concerto for myself. Finally, I adapted from Metastasio a short Italian cantata for solo voice, which had originally been written in honour of the seventh Name-day of the Emperor Charles, and as the word *Augusto* constantly occurred, I substituted for it *Adamo*, the Bishop's baptismal name. As I intended to show off the powers of my friend, Renner, I bore him specially in mind whilst I was composing. After making a fair copy of the text, I sent it to him secretly, when he was at Pesth, ordering two hundred copies to be struck off and bound there. The Bishop's copy was bound in violet satin, his own colour, and richly ornamented in gold. I got the packet in a week's time, but kept the secret entirely to myself.

The day came. The arrangement of the orchestra, the tasteful uniform of the musicians, which I had ordered, with the sanction of the Bishop — everything, in fact, combined to heighten the impression, and contribute to the pleasure of the crowded company of Hungarian nobles. Though the music of this cantata was my first unpretentious effort at a vocal work on a large scale, it was a success, and so far useful to me at least, that I learnt to avoid in future the hasty passages, unsuited to the text, which I had here introduced in abundance *sans rime et sans raison*.

I told Pichel one day that I was dissatisfied with the music, in relation to the text, so he altered the words for the songs and choruses, without changing a single note of my score, and made them suitable for the Church. This was the origin of the motets, which were frequently performed, turn and turn about, in the Cathedral.

The concert, with which I had intended to surprise the Bishop, was given on the following evening, and the very first bars of the symphony told him that it was a new work. Father Michael afterwards played a very beautiful concerto of his own. The Bishop's face beamed with satisfaction. Then Renner appeared on the platform. I gave the signal agreed upon, and the Court Steward stepped forward, and presented the Bishop with the copy of the Italian cantata bound in violet, on a silver salver, duplicates being distributed amongst the nobility. We had not played four lines when tears of joy were shining in the Bishop's eyes. He was overjoyed, as well as surprised, to hear nothing but new music the whole of the evening, and, rising from his chair, he thanked me in the most sympathetic language. So ended the *fête!*

A year passed, and we found that out of the sixteen thousand florins allowed for musical expenses, we had a surplus of fourteen hundred ; so it occurred to me that I might set up a small theatre at the Castle. The ground-plan and design were drawn by Neumann, the Bishop's architect, and the Bishop cheerfully approved of everything, especially as the sum required for the building, and for the four annual per- formances, did not exceed that which had been saved.

The Bishop's next Name-day happened to fall on one of the last days of the Advent season, when the performance of secular music, operas, and plays was forbidden by the Court, so I selected Metastasio's exquisitely beautiful oratorio, ' Isacco, figura del Redentore.' As Pichel was not strong in Italian, the Bishop himself undertook to translate the work into Latin. Following my advice, he made free use of the recitatives, but adopted strict metre in the airs. Whenever he had finished a scene, I was summoned to hear him read it ; he was constantly altering and improving, even after it was necessary, until at last, after the lapse of a month, he had completed the work so beautifully that the author himself would have confessed that the translation was a perfect rendering of the original text.

I was determined not to sit idle whilst the Bishop was engaged upon his translation, so I employed my leisure in quietly working at a Grand Concerto for eleven instruments, in the first allegro of which each soloist began with a passage for himself alone. Gradually three, five, seven, and finally nine parts were brought in. In the last solo all eleven took part, and at the end joined in a cadenza, which increased in strength as it went on. In the adagio the solo violin gave out a plaintive melody, and was joined by the other ten concerted instruments, first by four at a time, then by six, and finally by all; partly with different ornamentations, and partly with rich harmonic suspensions, the *ripieno* parts meanwhile accompanying with continuous *pizzicatos*. This slow movement died away with rich harmonies in a lugubrious strain at the end, but was interrupted by a fiery and brilliant Tempo di Menuetto, which was relieved by twelve *alternativi* (which in the present day are wrongly called trios), in all the allied keys. The twelfth *alternativo* was played by all the eleven solo instruments, and, after a cadenza and a changeful capriccio, closed with a shake in sixths played by nine instruments.

We worked hard at this Grand Concerto, often rehearsing in secret; and as I wished to have a surprise in store for the Bishop, I forbade any member of the orchestra to talk about it. I had hardly finished my task, when the Bishop gave me his libretto, and I set to work energetically at the oratorio. Meanwhile Neumann had not been idle, and as he came to an end about the same time that I did, we began to rehearse at the theatre.

My 'Isacco' was performed in the afternoon. As a proof of its universal popularity, I may mention that for four years it was given every Sunday in Lent, and always before a large audience. The actors, Renner, Mademoiselle Nicolini, the *castrato* who represented Sara, and Ungericht—everyone, including the boy who took the part of the angel, acted and sang most admirably. The scenic decoration consisted of a wood, in accordance with the directions of the poet. Abraham's house stood on one side of it. Even the costumes were made from models supplied by old drawings.

In return for this concert, the Bishop presented me with his favourite snuff-box, with two dozen kremnitzers inside it.

Now that we had a theatre, I thought of other spectacular devices   I asked the Bishop whether he would allow comedies, particularly at the time of the Carnival.

'Why not?' said he, 'so long as they do not contain any doubtful innuendoes.'

There was amongst the Bishop's cooks a man of the name of Sicca, who had lived some years in Italy.   He had rare histrionic powers. When he saw that we were building a theatre, he said to me:

'If you are thinking of getting up a farce, and want a comic man, I am at your service.   To be sure, I am not musical, but I have a good ear!'

Then he sang me some scenes out of the *opere buffe*, at which he had been present in Italy, with so much humour that I laughed aloud, upon which he went off into all sorts of absurdities in German, enacting clown, harlequin, pantaloon, and other comic personages in vogue at the time with such skill that I told him I was surprised that he had not turned actor by profession.   Whereupon he confided to me that he had upon one occasion left his trade and joined a travelling company, but they so scandalized him by their ill-conditioned life that he had retired in disgust, and gone back again to his old calling.

You may well imagine how pleased I was to acquire so useful an actor.

I patched together for the approaching Carnival a vaudeville of light songs, selected from those burlesques which I had formerly seen acted by Piloti's troupe at Schlosshof, and this was performed on the first day. Mademoiselle Nicolini and Sicca, the cook, would have compelled the veriest hypochondriac to laugh. The farce became so popular with the audience that they looked forward to Sunday with the greatest eagerness, because the theatre was always open on that day

In honour of the Bishop's birthday, I arranged a piece from two very old-fashioned farces, ' Frau Sibylla trinkt keinen Wein,' and ' Der Reich der Todten.' This was repeated on the first day of the Carnival, which occurred soon after. The Bishop gave a ball to his household on the Monday following, to which he invited the nobility of Grosswardein. I did not come away from this ball the same man that I went to it. I think the best plan will be to refer to this incident, though not at length.

Briefly, then, I scraped acquaintance with a nice graceful girl, Fräulein Furkowics, only daughter of the General-Perceptor, and fell in

love with her. On the death of her father, she
was to succeed to a fortune of twenty thousand
gulden. It was not this that attracted me; I
was caught by her bright, vivacious manner.
So out I came with my confession, and she
made hers at the second ball, the day afterwards. Nothing in the world could have been
quicker. Pichel followed my example with a
Fräulein Samogy, at the same time and under
similar circumstances. We mutually confided
our happiness to one another, and sighed
together in duets. The best of it was that the
two girls had been playfellows of old, and, as
they were very intimate, they made no secret
of their conquests. They had been together at
the boarding-school of the Ursulines at Pesth,
and had remained close friends ever since.

After languishing for over three months, I
reckoned for certain on my fair one's assent to
my offer, and made a serious proposal of
marriage. I did not hide from her that, in case
I made up my mind to leave Grosswardein, I
could find just as good a situation at Vienna.
She assured me of her joyful consent to this arrangement, only she feared that her father might
object. She said that, like most Hungarians,
he had a keen dislike of Germans; that he
held to his own caste, and had in his eye for a

son-in-law a *fade* young sprig of nobility, who
had already made a formal proposal for her
and been refused.

'He has a small landed property hereabouts,'
she said, 'only worth from five to six hundred
gulden ; but with what I shall inherit from my
mother, and other things, it would enable us to
get along pretty well. I advise you to put
forward the Bishop, before my father gives his
word to Lengyel ; perhaps that will help us,
for my father will certainly not refuse the
Bishop.'

I petitioned the Bishop next morning.

'Have you made matters straight with the
young lady ?' he inquired.

'Certainly,' I replied.

'Well, I will be your go-between ; but let
me first ask you a few questions, as your father
and your Bishop.'

Then, in a very rational and kindly way, he
tried to make me reflect. Afterwards he
asked :

'Well, what else troubles you ?'

I : 'Her father, like most Hungarians,
cannot endure the Germans.'

He : 'Oh, if that is all, I will say a few
words to him !'

I : 'Besides that, he wants to give her to a

nobleman, though his income does not at the most amount to more than five hundred florins.'

He: 'Her father, for a *Cassæ perceptor,* must be a bad hand at figures, if he cannot see that your earnings amount to twice as much.' (After a pause) : 'Well, I will look after this! Stay here, and you shall see for yourself whether I deserve any reputation as a matchmaker.'

The Bishop rang the bell, and sent for old Furkowics.   When he arrived, His Excellency stated the case with dignity and courtesy.

'What an unfortunate man I am!' cried the old hypocrite.   'Had Your Excellency only given me a hint a fortnight ago, I would cheer-fully have promised my daughter to so excellent a man' (*viro egregio* were the words used by the canting old rascal).   'But it is now too late, for this very day fortnight I promised my daughter to Herr von Lengyel, and Your Excellency yourself will see that I cannot take back my word, though I am inconsolable.'

Then the old dissembler turned to me, and addressed me also in Latin

'But you, you bad man, you who have been in and out of my house so often, why could not you speak sooner ?   Just see what mischief you have made by your silence ; for I am sure to get into hot water with my master by saying No!'

I answered him in the same language :

' It is in your own power to make it all right, if you will only dismiss Lengyel.'

I was too kind to give him the lie direct, and to say straight out that he had deceived us in this matter.

' What !' replied he.   ' Dismiss Lengyel ! Listen !' he continued in haughty tones.   ' You have yet to learn that every Hungarian, if he gives his word *sub fide nobili*, must abide by it ; if he breaks it, he ceases to be a Hungarian nobleman.'

Suppose the girl refuses her assent ?' interrupted the Bishop.

' Oh !' replied the old gentleman, ' she will be *obliged* to give her assent, unless she wishes to make out her father a liar and *disinherit* herself.   I suppose Your Excellency knows the Hungarian laws ?'   Feigning an air of great distress, he continued : ' I earnestly hope Your Excellency will not bear me a grudge, and will continue to allow me to stay in your service.'

At this point the cringing hypocrite was about to fall on his knees, when the Bishop stopped him, coldly observing ·*

' You had better drop that, unless you would

* The Bishop uses *Er* instead of *Sie* all through this speech.

have me think that you are overdoing your
part! You know as well as I know, and anyone possessed of reason knows, that family
affairs are not amongst the duties of an official.
You are father of your own child; I cannot
and will not command you in this matter.'

So saying, he dismissed him.

We stood and stared at one another for
over a minute. At last the Bishop said, smiling
rather bitterly ·

'You see, His Excellency the Bishop of
Grosswardein and his Right Honourable Conductor have had their noses pulled!'

'It is all very well for Your Excellency to
laugh,' I interrupted; 'but to me this insult is
no laughing matter. Did you not hear what
stress he laid upon the words *Hungarian
nobleman?*'

'I suppose I did; but do not quarrel with
me for saying that you ought to have thought
about this, before you carried matters so far
with the girl; for the Hungarian laws are clear
on the point, that if a daughter contracts a mis-
alliance, against the will of her noble parents,
they have the right to abandon and disinherit
her. Now,' he continued, 'I will give you
some paternal advice. Pull yourself together,
and remember that an artist like you, with a

good presence, character, and ability to get on and prosper, can find a hundred girls prettier and better off than this one. Let me advise you, as your Bishop, to yield to the will of Divine Providence. Who knows whether this marriage would have been for the best? It seems to me—nay, I firmly believe that Divine Providence has guided us in this matter! I see from your face that my good counsel falls on deaf ears; anyhow, promise me one thing, that to-day you will keep quiet!'

I promised him, and left, but went off to see Pichel.

'Good God!' he cried. 'What is the matter? You seem so put about.'

'It is all over with me. I have been refused.'

And then I told him the whole story.

'Alas!' he answered, with a sigh; 'your fate foreshadows a similar one for me to-day or to-morrow——'

'And what would you do in the emergency?' I interrupted.

'Well, what can I do?' said he, after a pause, except act as any rational man must—call philosophy in to help, and resign myself to my fate.'

'Oh, be hanged with your stoicism!' I called out petulantly. 'I come to you for comfort, and I am not to be put off with your chilling philosophy.'

I hurried away to my room, and after a few moments Pichel came to me.

'Come for a little walk,' he said 'I want to hear more about the matter ; perhaps I may be able to give you some good advice.'

It took a good deal to persuade me, but I went at last, and I must say thus much for this discreet and amiable young fellow, that his words had more weight with me than the wise sermonizing of the Bishop. At dinner I appeared far more cheerful than the latter could have supposed possible, for he openly expressed his astonishment at my good spirits. I candidly told him that, besides his fatherly admonitions, those of Pichel had had a great effect in calming me.

'Good!' said the Bishop. 'I thank him for that. Meantime, as there is nothing better than distraction for anyone in your state of mind, you have my leave to go to Vienna for three months' holiday. Promise me to come back when the time is over! I will order your horses as far as Pesth, and pay your travelling expenses from here to Vienna and back again—that is a matter of course.'

I accepted the offer, and amused myself to

my heart's content at Vienna ; besides that, it was a considerable advantage to me to be able to shake off my passion just then.

There was a capital *opera buffa* at Vienna in those days. One piece, ' Amore in Musica,' was my especial delight. I bought the printed libretto, in order to translate it into German. Soon after my return to Grosswardein, I set to work, wrote fresh music for it, and produced it on our stage. I brought back with me my youngest sister, by the way. She was a girl of sixteen, with a clear, but rather weak voice ; however, it was strong enough for us.

Five years did I spend in the enjoyment of all sorts of recreations. My favourite sport was hunting on the moors, though, alas! I ascribe to this a large share of the lameness in my feet from which I now suffer. My diversions came to an end all of a sudden.

CHAPTER XVII.

Scandalous gossip at the Court of Maria Theresa—The
Bishop's troubles—Dissolution of the band and chorus
—The story of Pichel's marriage.

NOT only was the Bishop fond of military
society on his own account, but the ever-memor-
able Empress, Maria Theresa, encouraged him
in it, for she once said to him at an audience,
' I shall be very grateful to you, if you and the
garrison of Grosswardein keep on good terms
with each other.' This hint was enough for
the Bishop, and he showed the garrison all
kinds of civility, from the General to the private.
Who would have thought that this would
cause the breaking-up of the Bishop's orchestra ?
At that time, it was a common thing to shift the
garrisons in Hungary, and it so happened that
the regiment at Grosswardein, after moving to
another province, was relieved by the Neuklein-
hold regiment, the Colonel of which belonged

to the princely family of Hohenlohe-Schillings-
fürst.   He was a man of twenty-seven years of
age, very fond of music and of the theatre, and
mad about dancing.   Naturally, the Bishop
showed him all the politeness due to a Prince,
and favoured his theatrical and musical tastes
in every way.   After attending the first concert,
he assured the Bishop, on his honour, that he
had not met with so fine a band and chorus
at the Courts of any of the Imperial Princes,
excepting those of Brunswick, Munich, Mannheim, and Stuttgart.   He was equally pleased
when he heard our opera, 'Amore in Musica,'
and sent me an invitation to dine on the
following day.   During the dinner, he told me
he had an equerry with a good tenor voice,
which he could turn to account on the stage,
and that he was at my service, whenever I
might want him to take a part.

There happened to be in the same regiment
another officer, Count Strasoldo, a first-rate
musician and a fine tenor; the Adjutant too,
Herr von Wreden, was a *basso profondo*, and
a capable actor; both of these volunteered their
services. Last of all, Countess Josephe, daughter
of Lieutenant-Colonel Count Figuemont, offered
to become a member of our company, by way of
return, as her father said, for the courtesies

shown by the Bishop to the whole garrison. She was a great beauty ; she had a pleasing voice, and she was very musical. You may well believe how eagerly I closed with these offers, and to what a pitch of perfection our private theatre attained. I have seen many theatres in the course of my travels in the provinces, but we were distinctly ahead of those at Grätz, Pesth, Pressburg, Brünn, etc.

I must frankly own that the knowledge I acquired in Grosswardein, and my continual efforts to write for the stage there, paved the way for whatever triumphs I was fortunate enough to achieve in my later days.

Of course I kept our actors in constant practice, to amuse our gracious Prince. For the same reason, the Bishop frequently gave balls and theatrical performances, not only during the Carnival, but in the summer season as well. The popular ' Isacco ' was only given during Advent and Lent. Grosswardein was consequently metamorphosed into a place well suited to anyone who cared for innocent pleasures.

One evening, when there was to be a ball at the Bishop's Palace, the Prince quietly prepared a surprise for the host, and summoning his officers, and the ladies of Grosswardein, got up an elegant masquerade, in the shape of a rustic wedding.

A week before the Prince's birthday (I think it was in the summer time), he invited the Bishop to meet a party of twenty-four friends at dinner. He was going, he said, to give a ball at the Rathhaus that same evening, to the great folk of Grosswardein, as his own rooms were not large enough.

The Bishop, wishing to make some return to the Prince for his impromptu masquerade, consulted me. I proposed a Turkish procession, and this was approved. The procession, accompanied by Turkish music, marched across the great Platz from the Bishop's Palace, where the masqueraders had assembled, and made for the hall of the Rathhaus.

Who would think that any villain could be found with hardihood enough to blacken so harmless a scheme?

The Bishop had one secret and malicious enemy amongst his Canons, who was highly incensed at an arrangement with which he really had nothing to do.

It should be understood that the Hungarian Bishops are not created by the vote of the Canons, as is usually the case, but that the King of Hungary has the direct power to nominate and institute the Bishop, as well as the Dean of the Cathedral. After the death of the Dean, the Empress, as Queen of Hungary, conferred the office upon a certain Count Kolonics, a member of one of the best families in Hungary. The above-mentioned Canon had reckoned on getting this post, but failing to do so, persuaded himself that the Bishop had recommended the Empress to appoint Kolonics, and that he had been passed over. Hence his hatred! What did the rascal do? He made a cat's-paw of one of the Queen's minions, through whom Her Majesty was informed that the Bishop not only supported a permanent theatre, but had comedies played at forbidden seasons, such as Lent and Advent —that not only balls, but masked balls, were given all through the year—that quite recently a procession of more than fifty masqueraders had marched in public from the Bishop's Palace across the Market Place, to the accompaniment of a noisy brass band, and that many such scenes as these had brought the greatest scandal on the whole body of the Clergy.

What a sneak that man was! He knew perfectly well that the Empress never allowed comedies or operas to be acted, either on public or on private stages, at sacred seasons—sacred compositions, such as oratorios, *were* allowed. ‘ Isacco ’ was an oratorio, so the first charge he made was a lie.   He also knew that the Empress had forbidden masks, but only those which veil the face, so he used the word *masqueraders* in order that Her Majesty might think they wore masks.   It was equally false to say that all the clergy had been scandalized, for, with the exception of the accuser himself, there was not one of the Chapter that had not seen the performances at our theatre, and instead of being annoyed, they were highly delighted.

What followed upon this denunciation ?   The Bishop received a private letter from Baron von Pichler, the Empress’s Private Secretary ; it ran as follows :

‘ I wish to inform Your Excellency, *sub rosâ*, that you have been denounced before the Empress.   These are the charges made against you : First, that comedies have been acted in the theatre attached to the Bishop’s Palace, during the seasons of Advent and Lent, in direct violation of the rules in all the Catholic and Imperial States ; secondly, that masked balls have been given throughout the year—not only that, but that you have organized a whole troop of masked persons, who marched from the Palace across the great Platz to the sound of a noisy band,—to the scandal of all the clergy of Grosswardein. Her Majesty will probably order that these matters should be investigated by a Commission, to be sent from Vienna. Your Excellency, however, may forestall this degradation, if you yourself remove the stumbling-block — the sooner the better! If Your Excellency does this of your own motion, I answer for it that Her Majesty will abate the inquiry.'

This document so intimidated the Bishop, a clever man under ordinary circumstances, that he lost his head completely. He locked himself in after dinner, and let no one come near him for quite four hours. At last, when evening fell, he summoned me, and said in a very depressed tone of voice :

'Would you drive with me to - morrow to Bellèniess ?'—a property belonging to the Bishopric, with a charming little house upon it.

'You may command me,' I answered.

'We will start punctually at six to-morrow morning,' he said.

We took our seats in the carriage just as the clock struck. We had driven nearly a mile, and the Bishop had hardly spoken a word, when the following conversation began :

I : ' I trust Your Excellency is not ill?'

He : 'Yes, my dear Karl, I am ill—not in body, but in mind.'

I : 'May I venture to ask what troubles Your Excellency?'

He : ' I have brought you with me on purpose to tell you about my trouble.' Then, drawing out Baron Pichler's letter · ' There, read it for yourself!'

I (after reading through the letter three times) · 'What profane calumnies! What shameful lies!'

He : ' Lies, you call it? Is it not true that plays have been going on at my theatre during the seasons of Advent and Lent?'

I : '*Distinguo!* Comedies, tragedies, dramas, and all secular pieces, are strictly forbidden at these seasons ; but oratorios are permitted. I myself have played in the orchestra when the very same oratorio, " Isacco," was given, with Bonno's music, in the middle of Lent, before the entire Imperial Court and all the chief nobility.'

He : 'Well, that may be! but is it a lie to say that I gave a ball at which there was a masquerade performance of a rustic wedding— that I myself organized a public procession in Turkish dress?'

I : 'With regard to the masquerade, it is

just as base a lie, for masks are strenuously
forbidden, without exception, in the Catholic
Imperial dominions ; but decent disguises, such
as domino, and rustic or national costumes, provided the face is seen, are permissible all the world
over.   I myself have constantly been present
at a *redoute* in Vienna, sometimes in a domino,
sometimes as a Spanish cavalier, sometimes as
a Venetian noble, sometimes as a Flemish boor.
Now, as we adopted the rustic costume at one
of our masquerades, and the national costume
at another, and as none of the dancers wore a
mask on his face, no royal command has been
violated, and therefore Your Excellency has
nothing whatever to answer for.'

He bit his lips and was silent.

I: 'What answer will Your Excellency make
to Baron Pichler ?'

He: ' I have already answered him.'

I: 'Am I right in assuming that you declared the charge to be false ?'

He: ' Oh no ; quite the reverse !'

I: 'What ?'

He: ' I thanked him for his kindly hint, and
told him that I had instantly made up my mind
to remove the stumbling-block, to put down
plays and balls, and to dismiss the greater part
of my band and chorus.'

I: 'Your Excellency must tear up that letter.'

He: 'It has gone already. I sent it to Vienna yesterday evening by special messenger.'

I: 'Alas, alas! Forgive me, Your Excellency, but you have been too hasty.'

He: 'Too true, alas! Oh that I had sent for you yesterday, before I wrote that unhappy answer! But now it is too late ; you yourself must see that nothing more can be done.'

I (shrugging my shoulders): 'Nothing more can be done, of course ; but what a pity that admirable band and chorus should be broken up !'

He: 'Yes, I agree with you. Let us drop the subject !'

We arrived at Bellèniess at three in the afternoon. After dinner the Bishop said :

'Come back to me in an hour's time, and you shall know what I have decided on, and take your measures accordingly.'

I came, and this was our conversation :

He· 'I want to stay here until my orchestra and chorus have all gone, for the dismissal of those dear good fellows would break my heart. I mean to retain you, Father Michael, and both my horn-players.'

I : 'Forgive me, Your Excellency, but what good should I be without the orchestra ?'

He · 'You will console me for the loss of it. You will be my friend until I die, and continue to enjoy the same salary and the same advantages as at present.'

I (after a pause) : 'Your Excellency will see for yourself that, without the band, my gifts as a violinist, as well as a composer, would be buried. Therefore I intend to travel, and to establish myself at some Court where I can find an opening.'

He : 'Your object is so praiseworthy, that it would be very wrong in me to dissuade you from following it up. Go ! Try your fortune in the world ; you will make a livelihood anywhere. God forbid that you should meet with any misfortune ; but if on your journeys you were to injure a hand or an arm, come to me ! As long as I live, you shall receive the same income that you have now, and I will take care that you have enough to live upon after my death. I expect you in my room here to-morrow morning at eleven o'clock, then you will know my arrangements about the band and chorus.'

I came on the day following, when the Bishop handed me over some papers in his own handwriting, and said :

'Here is the list of those whom I have dismissed. Here is an order to the house-steward to pay to each of my musicians, within three days, his quarter's wages, which are due five weeks hence, with an extra three months' wages in lieu of travelling expenses. Here is another order to my private secretary, to draw up a letter of dismissal, and a testimonial of good conduct, for everyone in the band, according to the enclosed formula ; he must send this back to me for my signature. Here is an order for my equerry to provide post-horses and good carriages as far as Pesth ; and here is a short note to my house-steward, who is to send Peter Hassmann, the cook, with his assistant and a servant, with food and wine, so that everyone may be properly provisioned on the six days' journey to Pesth. One thing more·no one of my old staff is to come and take leave of me—it would only open up the wound afresh. I will see no one but you, my son, and for the last time here in Bellèniess ! I allow every member of the band time enough to make arrangements for his journey, but I should be glad if you could one and all leave on the same day, the more so as I have made arrangements for your comfort and convenience as far as Pesth. To-morrow morning you will

go to Grosswardein and execute all my commissions. Come and see me once more before
you start !'

I promised I would, requesting to know if I
might tell the steward the reasons for the dismissal of the orchestra.

'By all means !' said the Bishop. 'Not only
may you tell the steward, but the whole town
may know of your justification, and that you
leave my service without a stain on your
characters.'

It is needless to say that my melancholy
news came like a thunderclap upon everyone in
Grosswardein. It vexed each member of the
disbanded orchestra, as well as the inhabitants
of the place. The musicians felt the loss of an
excellent master, the people felt that Grosswardein would be transformed back again into
the dreary desert it was before, since all these
pleasant entertainments, in which everyone was
able to take part, were to come to an end.
None was more inconsolable than my dear
Pichel ; but I had thought over his love affair
on my return journey fom Bellèniess to Grosswardein, and devised a plan, the successful
issue of which was still in the distant future.
Without saying a syllable to him about it, I
went to one of the Canons of the Cathedral on

the evening of my return, for I knew that he was an intimate friend of old Samogy, the father of Pichel's lady-love.   I soon succeeded in making this worthy ecclesiastic a partisan of Pichel, and he promised to do what he could for him.   Then I pointed out to him that time was precious, so we agreed to invite Samogy to dine on the following day, and I was to be asked to meet him.

During dinner, the Canon kept on filling his old friend's glass with the best tokay, and this nectar put the Herr Papa into the best possible humour.   The Canon watched his chance, and prevailed on Samogy to give his consent to his daughter's marriage with Pichel.   Overjoyed at the happy turn of events, I said :

'Herr von Samogy, of course you know the old proverb, *Qui cito facit, bis facit.* Why should we not make a match of it this very day?'

Samogy spoke good German; after all, he was not a determined enemy of our nation.

'As you will!' said he   'I don't mind.'

'Bravo!' exclaimed the Canon.   'The young people shall join hands at my house this very evening, and I will give you a good supper into the bargain.'

'All right!' said the old gentleman.

'Stop a bit!' said I. 'We must have a surprise for the young couple themselves. Not a word about your consent, please, Herr von Samogy, only bring your daughter to supper with His Reverence! I will bring Pichel.'

My suggestion was approved of, and we agreed upon a programme beforehand, to ensure the better success of the plan.

On my return home, I looked up Pichel, and proposed that we should take a walk together. He agreed to this, adding:

'I am at your service up to seven o'clock this evening, but then I must leave you, for I have promised to go to my Caton'—so he called his fair one.

As we walked along, the disconsolate lover poured out his troubles to me, and I affected to pity him, and said the same sort of thing to him that he did to me, when I was in the same sorrowful plight as himself. So artfully did I manœuvre our walk, that it seemed a pure accident that we should pass by the aforesaid Canon's house, as we went back. The Canon happened to be standing at the window, as we had agreed that he should. He returned our greetings, and called out:

'Which way are you going?'

'Home,' said I.

'Are we to believe the news which is all over the town ?'

'Alas! yes,' I answered.

'Well, just step up here, both of you, and tell me all about it!'

We did so.   I told him everything.   Pichel, getting restless, for it was nearly seven o'clock, was preparing to leave, when suddenly Samogy and his daughter came upon the scene.

'It is such a fine day,' said he, 'that my daughter and I could not deny ourselves the pleasure of paying Your Reverence a visit.'

'Bravo!' said the Canon.   'And now that we are such a jolly party together, I vote that we all stay for supper.'

We were agreeable.   The Canon rang the bell, and ordered a message to be sent to his cook, to prepare supper for five that evening.

At last we sat down to table.   All sorts of topics were discussed, and then our host quietly managed to turn the conversation upon a certain wedding, whereupon old Samogy cut in with a question :

'*À propos* of that,' said he, 'do you know that my daughter is also engaged?'

'You joke!' said the Canon.

'No, I am quite serious,' the old man answered.

'So sure as my name is Samogy, so surely is my daughter engaged to be married.'

Pichel and his 'Caton' turned pale.

'Who is the happy man, then?' said the Canon.

'Guess!'

The Canon ran over the names of six or seven young noblemen in or about Grosswardein, and purposely hesitated over each of his guesses, finally exclaiming, with pretended vexation

'Gracious me, why should I bother my head any longer? I don't care who it is!'

'Well,' said Samogy, 'then I must name the gentleman myself! It is none other than our friend Pichel here.'

The two lovers stared at the old gentleman, without uttering a word.

'Be hanged to you!' he cried. 'I believe you doubt the truth of it yourselves;' and rising hastily, he stepped between the lovers, who were sitting next to one another, clasped their hands together, and said, 'I give my consent, and my fatherly blessing into the bargain.'

Why attempt to describe the emotion on all sides? On resuming his seat, the old fellow said to them both :

'My dear children, we won't have a fine

wedding! Ready money in your pockets will suit you much better. As it is all to be quite quiet, I should be glad if the Bishop would dispense with the public asking of the banns.'

' I will manage that,' said I.

The Canon ordered up two bottles of his rare old tokay, and we sat at table, as happy as possible, until midnight.

Next morning, I summoned the former members of the orchestra, to discuss the time of leaving, which was fixed for ten days hence. On the same day I wrote to the Bishop, telling him of the time we should leave, and asked him to appoint an hour for my coming to Bellèniess to say good-bye. I also informed him that Pichel had been betrothed to Fräulein Samogy the night before, and asked him, on behalf of her father and also on account of our impending journey, to dispense with the usual banns. The Bishop wrote back that he expected me on the evening of the following Saturday. Would I bring Pichel, his bride, and her father with me, as he wished to bless the marriage himself?

The father, of course, was overjoyed at the honour done to his daughter and to himself.

On Saturday we drove to Bellèniess. Next morning, the Bishop officiated at Low Mass in his private chapel, and the marriage service took place afterwards. The bridal party, one and all, were invited to dine with His Lordship at noon. When we were sitting down, the bride and bridegroom opened their napkins, and each of them found underneath a roll of fifty ducats. On one the Bishop had written, with his own hand, *A small contribution to the table linen;* on the other, *For kitchen furniture.* The young people stood up, and kissed the Bishop's hand.

The guests were detained until six o'clock in the evening; then Pichel received his marriage certificate, and the Bishop dismissed him and the other guests, with the kindest expression of his good wishes. I was ordered to stay behind.

Everyone can imagine what a touching farewell it was. I will not describe it. I will only say that my patron asked me to tell him how I got on, and gave me a silk purse, which I was to use for my travelling expenses.

I had just begun to stammer forth my gratitude, but the Bishop stopped me. Folding his hands and breathing a silent prayer, he added his episcopal blessing, the last words of which were: *Descendat super te et maneat semper*, and without looking at me again, he disappeared into his bedroom.

I was so dazed that there was nothing for it but to rush into the open air, to get my breath again.   To this very day I cherish the memory of that solemn scene.

We took our departure from Grosswardein on the day we had settled to leave.   In such agreeable companionship, the journey as far as Pesth was pleasant enough.   I, my sister, Pichel, and his young wife, drove together in one carriage.   It took us a week to get to Pesth.   There the party broke up, each continuing his journey on his own account, except Pichel and myself, who determined to stay on for a few days, and then to go together to Vienna.   We hired a comfortable carriage, halving the expense.

CHAPTER XVIII.

Return to Vienna—Herr von Blanc, and the manufactures of Trieste—My excursion to Venice—The delightful storm—My adventure with a *danseuse.*

I HAD so large a circle of acquaintances in Vienna that I had no difficulty in getting four pupils for Pichel, each of whom paid him three ducats a month. Besides that, he had a certain income of twelve ducats, without reckoning what he made by private concerts, where I was able to be of great assistance to him ; so he and his young wife did not starve.

I determined to remain in Vienna over the summer, and to start on my grand tour in the beginning of autumn. A few days after my return to Vienna, I paid my respects to Count Spork, and he renewed the offer which he had made me before I went to Grosswardein ; but I was obliged to refuse it, on account of my intended tour, and it ended in my recommending

my friend Pichel.   By good luck, there was a
vacancy for the post of first violin at the
German Theatre, and Pichel got it.   The pay
was not more than four hundred and fifty florins
a year, but he accepted it eagerly.   His services
were only required of an evening, so he had the
whole day to himself, and could devote it to his
pupils.   I was happy in knowing that my best
friend was comfortably provided with a steady
income of one thousand and fifty gulden a year.

As for myself, my old friend Herr von Blanc,
Gouvernialrath at Troppau, made me a friendly
offer to join him as a fellow-traveller to Trieste ;
which offer I accepted.   He had come to
Vienna unexpectedly, having been commissioned by the Empress to examine and
report upon the manufactures of Trieste ; and
as his business there detained him for at least
three weeks, I determined to make an excursion to Venice alone, and to pay a visit to my
former chief, Count Durazzo.   The wind was
so much in our favour that we reached Venice
in thirteen hours, but to my great disappoint-
ment, the Count and his wife had just started
for Milan. Ascensiontide was over.   Of the
four operas given at that season, three had
completely failed, and the other was only
struggling on.   I thought it so commonplace

that I merely allude to it, for I never cared to hear it again.

The absence of the Count, the vexation of not hearing a good opera, finally, the unbearable smell of the lagoons in summer, disgusted me so much, that I took ship for Trieste on the fourth evening after our arrival. The wind was very unfavourable, and next day it increased to a storm, driving our ship many miles out to sea. Who would have thought that this adverse wind, so far from fretting or even terrifying me, would be the very thing I wanted, and would bring about a happy incident in my career?

One of our cabin passengers was a pretty *ballerina*, a Venetian by birth, from eighteen to nineteen years of age, with large, black, fiery eyes. I could not help staring at them; to look away was impossible. Such was the simple beginning of my love adventure with this bewitching coquette, and I was a lost man from the first moment she stepped on board. Besides her servant, she was attended by her 'mother,' for Italians give that name to old ladies, who are paid to act the part for the sake of conventionality, and personate the character in society, though, when alone with their mistresses, they are only chambermaids. The lady being engaged as *première danseuse* at

Vienna, I had no difficulty in scraping acquaintance, and offered to do what I could for her in my native place.   It was her first visit to Germany, she said, so she graciously accepted my offer, and was candid enough to confess that she was delighted to fall in with a friend whom she could implicitly trust from the first.

I dare say I was weak ; let others boast of their strength !   In the space of less than two hours, we were older friends than sensible folk, who do not sail so fast into new relationships, would have been in two months.   Anyhow, we were already on the borderland of brother and sister.   Who would not have wanted a sister like that?   She had a charming face ; her figure was slender and well proportioned ; her *naïveté* and humour were irresistible in her Venetian dialect.   One must at least insist on the freedom of relationship !   I purposely conceal her name ; that and her talents became subsequently only too well known.

Next day, the wind and the storm increased, and the ship rolled so heavily that the poor girl could not stand, so I was compassionate enough to clasp her in my arms, and the timid creature yielded so readily that I should like to see the man who could have remained an indifferent fellow-passenger !

The storm had carried us so far out of our
way, that four days elapsed before we reached
Trieste. Of course I extemporized a plan to
put her up at the same hotel where Blanc and
I lived. She fell in with it ; she did more,
she let herself be persuaded to stay three
days at Trieste, and there on dry ground
the play went on, the prologue of which had
begun on the open sea. We dined together
in the middle of the day, together in the
evening, so as to ensure meeting as often
as possible. Blanc executed his mistress's
commissions, whilst I attended on my queen at
home. She asked me to get her a new and
comfortable travelling-carriage. Next morning
I found one ready made, and came to terms
with the owner ; but in order to prolong my
stay for a few days at Trieste, I artfully let her
understand that the carriage would not be ready
to start for a week, so she was forced to agree
to remain on for that time. Those six days
seemed but six hours to me in my dream of
bliss ; but I must be careful about what I
say.

She went to Vienna before me. Blanc's
business kept him eight days at Trieste ; that
finished, I joined her. How I cursed all the
manufactures and the commission during that

interval ! for I was pining for the moment when I and my charmer were to meet.   It was rather late in the evening when we got to Vienna, but I could not rest for a moment till I had inquired where the dear creature lived.   She, too, was overjoyed to meet me earlier than she expected, and, of course, I was obliged to stay to supper with her.

About ten days after my return, she made her *début* in a new ballet.   Her beautiful figure and rare talent excited the public to the highest pitch of enthusiasm.   No singer, no dancer had ever met with so triumphant a reception. Who, unless he has tasted the bliss already, can imagine the pleasure of knowing himself to be favoured by such a creature ?   Her dress set off her charming figure, which might have been a subject for Pygmalion.   When she was surrounded by picturesque groups, her expressive face grew more radiant as she danced, and she bewitched not only the dandies and the fops, but also well-conditioned youths, middle-aged men, and old fogies.   Let him who can picture the happiness of the lover who says to himself, ' See the beauty there, for whom the minions of Fortune, with their carriages and their Orders, are fighting ; to flirt with whom, for one short hour, they would stake their last farthing ; who would tempt a saint — that exquisite creature *is thine !*'

My reader will forgive me if I change colour even now at these recollections, when, at sixty years of age, I paint the dream of my youth with colours still so fresh ! I was silly—guilty, if you will have it so—that I know well enough ; but let him condemn me that has the heart !

I had intended to keep my *liaison* a close secret, but it was utterly impossible ; so I confided to one of my most reliable friends the story of my good fortune, as I, donkey that I was, called this very immoral action, feeling sure that he would give me joy of my triumph, and perhaps actually be envious of me. But imagine my surprise, when this estimable friend (why should I suppress my guardian angel's name ?—it was Herr von Demuth) listened to and condemned my confession, rebuking me in scathing fashion.

'Shame on you, Ditters—you, a man of thirty years of age, without a moment to lose in your career as an artist ! You to hang on to a girl— and *such* a girl as this—at the risk of your future, your health, your honour ! Take my advice—be a man. Tear yourself away from the arms of this wicked enchantress—shake yourself free from a degrading passion. Go out into the world! Choose any Court you please where you can make a livelihood, and stay there. Then marry a virtuous girl, and have children. If you reject my advice, we part company.'

Shocked as I was by these words, and ready to rise in revolt at a moment's notice, when I came to cooler reflection afterwards, the honest principles of my good friend convinced me. Peace be to his ashes! His few but impressive words sank deep into my soul; the scales fell from my eyes, and—I saw the siren no more. I learnt from my friend, a year and a half afterwards, that she had had an intrigue with the well-known and wealthy Count N. N., a man of very distinguished family. She had ruined him so completely that he had had to part with his sumptuous carriage, and was now trudging the streets on foot, a pensioner on the smallest pittance contributed by the charmer's other admirers. All this had come to the ears of the Empress, and one night the *signora prima ballerina* was arrested by the police and carried off, bag and baggage, to the borders of Italy.

CHAPTER XIX.

Count Lamberg—The Prince-Bishop of Breslau—My engagement—The hunt—I become *Eques Aureatus*—
Frederick II. at Rosswald—Count Hoditz—The Crown
Prince's kindness to me—My promotion to the office
of Forstmeister.

ON my journey to Trieste, I had become acquainted with Count Lamberg, President and
Chief of the Imperial Duchy of Silesia. He
had come to Vienna from his estate near
Laibach, on the way to Troppau, to his depart-
ment, and I paid my respects to him. Hearing
I was about to travel, he asked me whether I
would accompany him to Troppau, and include
it in my last excursion.

'Then,' he added, 'you could go to Warsaw,
Danzig, Hamburg, the Netherlands, Holland,
England, and France, and return by the Papal
States, etc.'

I liked the idea, and four days afterwards we
drove off in his carriage together. He was

rich, and having no children, he outdid everyone in Troppau in his extravagance. Grand
dinners, assemblies, and concerts were of frequent
occurrence. He was not the only nobleman, for
there was a Count Chorinsky, like himself a
large proprietor in Austrian and Prussian Silesia,
who had a fine orchestra. With the aid of these,
and other musicians in Troppau, I got together
a small though quite adequate band.

The Prince-Bishop of Breslau arrived at
Troppau soon after we came there. He was
then residing on his episcopal estates in Imperial
Silesia, but he wanted to pay a visit to the Head
of the Province. A concert was given in his
honour, and the Prince, when he had complimented me warmly on my playing and my
composition, invited me to dine with him three
days afterwards. He was naturally very talka-
tive, and during dinner engaged me almost
exclusively in conversation, cross-examining
me, as a musical enthusiast would, about the
whole course of my life, and discussing my
plans for the future. He made no secret of
the fact that in former and better days, when
he lived at Breslau, he had not only had a fine
orchestra in his employ, but numerous *castrati*,
and amongst them the famous Quadagni.

The story of the Prince-Bishop's quarrel with

Frederick II. will be familiar to many readers, but the greater part of the printed record was published in Prussia, and everything is so exaggerated and overdrawn, that I do not think it superfluous to tell the story as I heard it from the lips of Count Lamberg.

The Prince-Bishop was a member of the distinguished family of Count Schafgotsch. His father, the Head Landsdirektor, was like a Viceroy in Silesia, when that province was still the sole property of Austria. He resigned when Frederick II. first took possession of Silesia in 1740, and by permission of the King, retired to his great estate of Warmbrunn in the Riesengebürge, where he resided for many years. The King, diplomatic enough to keep in with the Silesian nobles, as well as their subjects, and with the Catholics in particular, conceived a great affection for his son, who was at that time a canon and prelate. He made him his Coadjutor, and subsequently Bishop of Breslau, in succession to Sinzendorf, Bishop and Cardinal, who died shortly afterwards. To this office two titles are invariably added, that of the Reigning Prince of the Principality of Neisse, and of Duke of the Duchy of Grottkau. The King was on such friendly terms with the Bishop, that he never let a year pass, without inviting

T

him to stay some months either at Berlin or at Potsdam. His confidence remained unimpaired for years and years, and still survived at the beginning of the Seven Years' War. The battle of Kollin, in which the King was beaten, took place after the march of the victorious army into the heart of Bohemia, when the Imperial troops had been forced to fall back upon Prague, and Prague, and finally Austria itself, was menaced. The fortune of war turned so much in favour of the Austrians, that they not only expelled the Prussians from Bohemia, but pressed on into the heart of Silesia, and, after the battle of Breslau, again made themselves masters of that capital. Everyone, the King himself included, believed Silesia to be lost for ever. Every Catholic priest and subject, who on account of his religious creed had always wished well to the Emperor, rejoiced over the event, and the Prince-Bishop, if rather over-hasty in expressing his delight, made no sort of secret about it.

Meanwhile, most of the Imperialists at Breslau, who mistrusted the Prince-Bishop as being a former favourite of the King, advised him to withdraw to Rome for so long as the war lasted. Whilst he was there, the luck changed again, so he returned, and went to Nikols-

burg and to Moravia, where he awaited the issue
of events. Here he wrote to the King, availing
himself of every possible argument in favour of
another reconciliation, but he received in return
that well-known letter, in which His Majesty
not only rebuked his ingratitude, but abused
him as a disloyal traitor, whom he would not
tolerate in his States, though otherwise he left
him to the reproaches of his own conscience.
The Prince-Bishop asked the Imperial Court
to intercede, and the King thereupon yielded
so far as to allow him to return to Silesia.

But there was no precedent to show that
Frederick II. ever came to terms again with
anyone who had once fallen out of his favour, so
it was hopeless for the Prince-Bishop to expect
any reconciliation. Even at the borders, he
was met with an order not to come to Breslau,
and told that he was to reside at Oppeln, a
mean, wretched little town in North Silesia.
No lodgings were to be had, so he was quartered
in a few miserable rooms in the Convent of the
Minorites. Though he had been officially told
that he was not to consider himself a prisoner
of State, he fared almost as badly. For the
first quarter he drew his full revenue from
Prussian Silesia, but for the second only a half,
for the third three-fourths, and for the last the

whole of his income was confiscated. Thus it came about that his powers as a Bishop were so limited that, without the approval of the Minister for Silesia, he could not fill up any vacant benefice.

The Prince-Bishop's affairs went from bad to worse. Seeing that, so long as the King lived, there was no chance of their getting better, he gave up everything in that neighbourhood, his income as well as his own valuable furniture, and withdrew to Imperial Silesia, where he had been living for nearly two years solely on the income of his property on this side of Johannisberg, which brought him from thirteen thousand to fourteen thousand gulden in all, whereas in former years it had amounted to upwards of one hundred thousand gulden.

On one occasion—after my return to Troppau from a great *fête* at Rosswald, on the property of the celebrated Count Hoditz—I found Padre Pintus, the Prince-Bishop's confessor, who had been specially sent to ask me if I would make up my mind, on the strength of a handsome honorarium, to spend the next winter at Johannisberg. Would I be, peradventure, to the Prince what David was to Saul when, harp in hand, he cheered the melancholy hours of the King?

'To be sure,' said he, 'the Prince has no orchestra, but still there are a few musical servants, secretaries, and officials in Johannisberg; we might get together a small orchestra of eight, without wind-instrument players. Besides that, I am commissioned by the Prince to offer your servants free lodgings and maintenance in the Castle, besides a salary of twenty-five ducats a month. You must let me know your decision within three days.'

I considered the matter during the interval, and then bound myself to remain at Johannisberg for seven months—*i.e.*, from November 1 to the last day of May, 1770.

I must not omit to mention one incident of that time, for it caused me to give up the whole plan of my journey, and more than that, it had a very marked influence on the rest of my career.

The Prince-Bishop had arranged for a three days' stag-hunt in September. I was invited, and so were Count Larisch, Count Hoditz's son-in-law, and the Gouvernialrath von Blanc, whom I have mentioned before. I happened to have a pair of good rifles, and was so fortunate, on the first day, as to kill seven fine stags, two roebuck, and a brace of foxes. At early dawn, next day, we were in the saddle,

with five good hours of riding before us ere
we could arrive at the trysting-place in the high
mountains. The hunt lasted until late in the
evening, and we camped out all night on the
mountains in a huntsman's cottage, erected on
purpose. Guests and riders included, we were
a party of fifty, ranged round a fire in the midst
of us, which it was the huntsmen's duty to keep
going. During great part of the night I talked
with the Chief Whip and his underlings, whose
curiosity culminated at last in comical surprise
and admiration, for—owing partly to my own
experiences at Schlosshof, partly to good sporting books and the society of the head-keeper
there—I had come to know something about
forestry and sporting matters, and had afterwards busied myself with hunting, and shooting
too, at Grosswardein. On the third day the
hunt extended to the larger covers, and again
I succeeded in making many good shots at roebuck and foxes.

Before dinner, the Prince asked each of his
guests what he had killed. When my turn
came, the Chief Whip prevented me by
narrating one and all of my heroic deeds, and
ended his speech thus :

'Your Highness may well believe not only
my evidence, but that of all my comrades and

beaters, who vouch for the fitness of this gentleman to fill the first place at any Court as Huntsman or Forester.'

These words were not spoken in vain, for the result was that, after a long interval, I was offered a post for which some knowledge of woods and forests was a requisite condition, and I became a permanent fixture here, as I shall have to tell later on.

On the same day the conversation shifted to the journey which I had made in Gluck's company, and the Prince asked me how he had acquired the title of Chevalier, and whether he belonged to the nobility. I told him all I knew. He became thoughtful, and withdrew from the party. After supper he asked me whether I had written any masses in Italian, and any songs. I said 'Yes'; whereupon he pressed me very politely to let one of my best masses be scored, besides an Italian air, a violin concerto, and a symphony—all of which I was to send to Johannisberg. I made great haste to despatch my parcel from Troppau as soon as possible, before I had paid the copyists. The Prince answered me that he had received the consignment, but that I had forgotten to enclose the copyist's bill; he would let me have twenty ducats to pay it. Then he announced that, on the last day of October, I might expect a carriage and horses at Troppau, to carry me off to Johannisberg.

Arrived there, I found such a piteous state of things, with an orchestra consisting of ten persons, myself included, that I was downright disgusted; but what was to be done? I had to put up with it. And by dint of incessant practice and hard work, I succeeded so far that, after one month, our performance was just bearable.

On the morning of New Year's Day, Padre Pintus and I visited the Prince, to offer him our congratulations as usual. Think of my astonishment when, after I had made my bow, he drew out of his desk a piece of parchment, folded in four, and addressed me thus :

' Dear Ditters, I have been commissioned from Rome to make you a New Year's present in the shape of a diploma, sent by Cardinal Archinto, by virtue of which you have been made a Knight of the Golden Spur, in consequence of his approval of the music that I sent him.'

With these words, the Prince took from a little case the Cross of the Order. It was attached to a red ribbon, and whilst he was putting it on with his own hands, he said laughingly :

'Now you are just as much a Chevalier as Gluck himself, and whenever you are in Rome, you have as much right as every born Chevalier of the first rank to enter the Pope's palace, and to be present at every public function as " *Eques aureatus ac Sacri Palatii et aulæ Lateranensis Comes.*" '

Think of my radiant happiness at being invested by the Prince, who had had everything in hand a fortnight before, but had postponed the ceremony until now, that he might have a surprise for me on New Year's Day !

Still, in spite of all the kindness, graciousness, and sociability for which I was indebted to him, I felt wearied by the daily routine of Johannisberg, and I longed for the end of May, so as to get quit of my engagement, and be ready to start on my summer journey. But the Fates were against this, for I unexpectedly received an invitation from Count Hoditz to visit him at Rosswald, and I could not possibly refuse it, so once more I had to put off my trip to the autumn.

The cause of the invitation was King Frederick II.'s proposal to visit the Count at Rosswald. He had already made his acquaintance during the Seven Years' War, and esteemed him very highly as a philosopher. It is well known that the Emperor, Joseph II., had paid the King a visit at Neisse, in 1769, and the King, having promised to return it in the summer at Neustadt, near Olmütz, in Moravia, wrote that he hoped to make arrangements *en route* for passing a night at Rosswald, on his journey to and fro. The reason the Count asked me was, that I might help him with some plays which he was getting up, so I appeared on the scene a fortnight before the King's arrival, and did my best to arrange everything in conformity with the ingenious plans of my excellent patron.

The King arrived at Rosswald punctually at four o'clock on the afternoon of the day agreed on. He was attended by the Crown Prince, Prince Frederick Augustus, Prince Leopold of Brunswick (who was afterwards drowned at Frankfort-on-the-Oder), and General Lentulus.

Soon after the appearance of these grandees, the Count proposed a walk in the garden, during which the guests were surprised with little *spectacles* here and there; for instance, a ballet in the open air, the subject of which was the transformation of Daphne into a laurel; a Druid's Feast; and in especial a City of Pigmies, which greatly delighted the King. He went to bed at sunset, but the suite remained.

The two sides of the Chinese garden, which were brilliantly illuminated by order of the Count, bore a transparent inscription, ' The Austrian and The Prussian Grotto.' The Count asked the Crown Prince in which of the two he would like to hear a little concert, and he replied :

' To-day I have the pleasure of being in the Austrian States, so I should prefer to hear the concert in the Austrian Grotto.'

Preparations were made accordingly. The orchestra was a very fair one, for I had fused together the two small bands of Count Hoditz and Count Chorinsky. My symphony was beginning when the Princes entered, and after that I played a concerto. When it was over, the Crown Prince said :

' Your name is known to me already, and so are your gifts. I possess several of your compositions, and I am glad to make your personal acquaintance.'

Later on he asked me to perform again, and after I had played a sonata with real enthusiasm, he paid me so many compliments that I blush to repeat them. You must know the man to be able to appreciate his delicate kindness towards those whom he respected !

Very early on the following morning, the

King, accompanied by a small suite, drove to Neustadt, and a few days afterwards returned to Rosswald, and dined there. After dinner the Crown Prince sent for me, and asked me about the shows I was preparing. I told him everything, but he asked me to substitute a concert, at which I was to play. I ' did play three times, and when it was over, Count Hoditz came out of the King's rooms, and proposed some short spectacular scenes; but the Prince declined, urging as his reason that the King had arranged to start at two o'clock in the morning. Then he beckoned me to the window, and graciously questioned me on various subjects relating to art and to well-known artists. Finally, when I told him of my intended journey, he pressed me very courteously to stay at Berlin, where he would try and make my visit as agreeable as possible.

The King behaved most generously to the Count, presenting him with a large, square, golden snuff-box, set with brilliants, and adorned with his own portrait. Enclosed was a folded document, with an inscription written by the King himself:

'On presentation of this document, our Minister of State will pay 10,000 thalers to Count Albrecht Hoditz.

'(Signed)   FRIEDRICH.'

I lingered on at Rosswald another two days, and then went back again to Johannisberg, where I began to make serious preparations for my journey in October. I meant to go first to Berlin, whither the Crown Prince had just invited me so graciously and kindly. But Fate had ordained otherwise.

One day I was summoned by the Landeshauptmann, Baron Zedlitz, a distant relative of the Prince-Bishop, and, after many pretty speeches, he informed me of the Prince's wish to retain me in his service for the rest of my life. I refused; my reason being that during the Prince's lifetime I should be wasting my best years, without the consolation of realizing a competence for my old age.

'That,' he replied, 'is all arranged. The Prince wishes to confer on you the post of Forstmeister in the Principality of Neisse on-this-side, having written testimonials from the Chief Whip and everyone under him as to your proper qualifications. The Cathedral Chapter is prepared to confirm your appointment.'

So saying, he drew out a written document, in which it was clearly stated that the Cathedral Chapter was fully disposed to recognize the validity of the transaction. This recogni-

tion included, *eo ipso*, the confirmation of the
appointment, even after the death of a Prince-
Bishop, in the usual terms :

' These are to show that A. B., after the
death of the Prince-Bishop for the time being,
is immediately bound to us, until such time
as we assign him over to the Bishop next in
succession.'

I was offered a handsome salary of six
hundred florins, and nine hundred in stock,
making fifteen hundred florins in all. Besides
tha, there was the reversion of the post of
Amtshauptmann, when the first vacancy should
occur; this would greatly improve my position
hereafter, and ensure my retention of all the
emoluments in the way of board, maintenance,
etc., which I had hitherto received.

So far so good! But the miserable state of
the Prince's orchestra, if I may call a mere
handful of people by such a name, was the one
thing which made my life unendurable. However, it was pointed out to me that one half of
my former income of twelve hundred florins
was derived from the Prince's rents, and now
that the price of timber had risen, there was an
overplus of nine hundred florins, making a clear
profit of fifteen hundred to the Prince, which he
was ready to spend on the improvement of his

band. He would further supplement this with another sum of nineteen hundred florins, which had been intended for the formation of a small stud, and the reconstruction of a zoological garden, which had fallen into decay. Also it should be arranged that such of his servants as were not musicians should be provided with other posts, and musical substitutes found to succeed them. This satisfied me, and gave me good hope.

Interests easily clash in a thing of this kind, so Baron Zedlitz and I went to the Prince, and discussed every point with him. When everything was settled, I formally and gratefully accepted my post, and from that time I abandoned the idea of my journey altogether. On the following day, I received the title-deeds of my appointment, and a letter confirming the amount of my salary. These documents were afterwards officially confirmed by the Cathedral Chapter of Breslau. Soon after that, I took an oath of fidelity, in the presence of all the huntsmen assembled. The Landeshauptmann introduced me to them as their actual chief, and they also had to take the same oath to me. And so it came about, that I was installed as Forstmeister of the Principality of Neisse on-this-side.

CHAPTER XX.

The oval theatre in the tower—My oratorio 'Davide'—
My comic opera, 'Il Viaggiatore Americano'—Demoiselle Nicolini—My honourable marriage.

THOUGH I made all my arrangements then and
there, without losing a moment, there was a
long interval before I got my very small
orchestra into some sort of order. It consisted
of seventeen persons, myself included. Eleven
received an ordinary salary, but the rest were
on the footing of common household servants.

My hobby-horse neighed and jibbed rest-
lessly, until I made an effort to mount and
master him—in other words, I was tormented
by the idea of building a private theatre.
Where was the site to be found?

Nothing could be done with the wretched
old Castle. The inscription on it ran thus:
'*Johann Turso, Bishop of Breslau, after re-
storing out of his own pouch this Castle, ruined*

by the tooth of Time, dedicated it to St. John the Baptist, and gave it the name of Johannes, in the Year of our Lord 1509.' So you will understand that there was not much to help me, in a Castle that had already been ruined by *the tooth of Time* in the year 1509, and was supposed to have been built in the ninth or tenth century. But where there is a will, there is a way.

Adjoining the Castle buildings stood a massive round tower, which, in its larger diameter, measured about eight *Klafter.** I turned my mind to this. It was only a question of reducing it to the level of the other rooms, and roofing it in as an oval hall. The Prince, when the matter was laid before him, thought the plan feasible, and asked for the estimate, which was not very high. All the necessary materials could be found on the episcopal estates, and as every subject was bound to assist him gratis in the building of the Castle, the Prince had only to pay the tradespeople. In short, the theatre rose like magic, and before the middle of autumn, the *salon* was finished and painted. It was so well adapted for hearing, that even now I would advise any nobleman with an orchestra of his own to copy it in

* About forty-eight feet.

respect of height, size, and shape.   He will find that this method of construction largely contributes to strengthen the sound, without adding to the echo.

We set up our theatre in this hall, and I prepared to get my company together.   I wrote to my bosom friend Pichel in Vienna, and he sent me Renner, now a widower, his daughter, and Ungericht, who was wandering about in search of a livelihood.   The Prince was not only content that I should summon my sister, but he gave her a room at the Castle, and a place at his own table.

Now I had once more a troupe that could do me honour.   Padre Pintus was a good Italian poet.   He wrote for the Lenten season ' Davide,' a beautiful oratorio, and for the first of May a comic opera, ' Il Viaggiatore Americano.' Mademoiselle Nicolini had greatly improved in every way since I last saw her ; she was a favourite with everyone.   She played the part of David in a masterly fashion.   And what part did I play ?   And how ?   That my readers shall soon learn !

Here I ought really to begin a new chapter, for I am talking of an important stage in my career; but as there is no romance nor adventure connected with it, nothing but what is common

to ordinary citizens, I will continue my narrative
without interruption.

I used to give the worthy Nicolini a lesson
every day. Did I fall in love with her? If
you will have it so, I did ; but that is not
exactly what I meant to say ! I had many oppor-
tunities of discovering both her good qualities
and her solid character, so I made up my mind
to come out boldly with an offer of marriage,
though I resolved to keep it to myself yet
awhile, until I had satisfied myself that I could
live happily with her, and she with me. When
at last I was clear upon that point, I one
morning made her the offer, asking her at the
same time to take as long an interval as she
chose for reflection—a year if she liked ! She
answered that she needed no time for reflection,
provided she had the consent of her stepfather,
Herr Renner. There was not the slightest
difficulty about that Then I proposed to shift
the scene to the Prince's apartments, and there,
in the presence of himself and my *fiancée*, to
pledge my troth. This done, the business
was settled off-hand. The Prince was quite
ready to dispense with the banns, and to have
the service performed on the following Sunday.
But, as I thought it more honourable for myself
as well as for my bride, not to claim the dis-

pensation, the wedding was fixed for seven months later, at which the Prince was greatly pleased, as was his sister-in-law, the Countess Schafgotsch, who happened to be in Johannisberg at the time. My bride became a constant guest at the Prince's table, and he kissed her on the lips.

I was married in the Castle chapel on March 3 of the following year, having loyally stuck to my duty since the previous July. The Prince gave us five rooms in the Castle, and presented me with a letter, stating that all the furniture and fittings were my sole property.

CHAPTER XXI.

Florian Gaszmann is made Kapellmeister on horseback—
He tries to lead me on to thin ice—Malice the origin of
my best oratorio, 'Esther.'

A YEAR after my marriage, I made an excursion
to Vienna. I called upon my friends and
patrons there and, amongst others, upon Herr
Florian Gaszmann, who, during my absence,
had become Imperial Kammer- and Hof-
Kapellmeister. I wanted to give him joy of
the appointment, which Gluck had vacated by
his own wish, receiving a pension of two
thousand florins.

'Do you know, too,' said he, 'that I was
made Hof-Kapellmeister on horseback?'

'How so?' said I.

'The Emperor, as is well known, always
consults his own wishes in making official appointments,' said he, 'and frequently runs
directly counter to the advice and suggestions

offered by others.   Ritter, my predecessor, died early, at eight o'clock in the morning. The Emperor heard the news two hours later, and took his usual ride in the Augarten an hour after.   I chanced to meet him on the Graben. He had already gone a little way beyond me, when he came suddenly to a stop, and called out : " I will tell you a piece of news—Ritter is dead!"   I replied that I was aware of the fact an hour ago.   Then he said, rather crossly : " But I am sure you do not know that you are Hof-Kapellmeister in his place ;" and with that he rode away.'

In the preceding Lent, Gaszmann had written an oratorio, ' Betulia Liberata,' the words by Metastasio, for the benefit of the Institute for Widows of Musicians ; it was performed with an orchestra of two hundred persons.   I was told that it had made a great hit, so I asked the composer's leave to look through the score. He consented, and I had just been sitting a couple of hours over the work, and had discovered many beautiful passages in it, when Gaszmann paid me a visit in return.   I happened to have some of the scores of my choral music upon the table ; he looked them through, and said many pretty things about them, but I had my misgivings as to his entire sincerity.   Meantime, as we were in the full tide of compliment, and I wished to return his politeness, I said ·

' If I had known when your oratorio was to be given, I should never have grudged the expense of a journey from Silesia to Vienna, merely for the sake of hearing such a masterpiece !'

' Well,' said he, ' it entirely depends on you, whether a still greater pleasure be not in store for you, if you consent to write an oratorio for the Widows, and conduct it here in person ?'

' What on earth puts that into your head ?' said I ' To write a grand oratorio for Vienna ! You rate me very high. I to appear after Hasse—after you !'

' Yes,' said Gaszmann ; ' and to cut us both out !'

This he said with such pointed irony in voice and face, that I could not fail to recognize the rogue underneath. It annoyed me, and I said nothing. He misconstrued my attitude, and thought he had got the better of me.

' Certainly,' he said, breaking the silence, ' it wants a little courage to approach such a precipice. Do just as you like ; if you have not the heart——'

' Oh, Heaven forbid !' I exclaimed, with rather sulky defiance. ' You are quite mistaken ! I have plenty of courage, and I take

you at your word. You have offered me an
oratorio.   I thank you for the distinction.
Here is my hand—I will write one !'

'Bravo !' said Gaszmann, with strange friend-
liness; 'that's all right.   I will send you the
works of Metastasio——'

'I have them,' I replied.

'Or those of Apostolo Zeno, so that you can
take your choice.'

'I have those also, but I expect, with such
a large choir, choruses would be very effective,
and, as there do not happen to be enough of
them in any of the oratorios which you have
proposed, I will order a libretto from a good
friend of mine, who knows Italian well, and is
a poet into the bargain.   I shall have up to
next Advent to write the music, and will conduct it here myself.'

Then you must give me your word of
honour,' he replied. 'to save me from getting
into disgrace with the Emperor, to whom I shall
have to announce your coming beforehand.'

I assented to this, and he left.

That same day I saw Pichel, and told him
all that had passed, and also of what I had
undertaken to do.   Then he said, in a tone of
warning :

'Don't trust Gaszmann ; he is a downright

humbug, and is laying a snare to catch
you.'

'The deuce he is!' I replied. 'I will go
back to him this very day, and cancel the
agreement.'

'Do not so! I know too well how gifted
you are, not to have a well-grounded hope of
your success.'

'But how do you know that he does not
mean to act fairly by me?' I asked.

'Because,' replied Pichel, 'I have shown
him several of the scores that you composed
at Grosswardein, and he rejected them all.'

'But then he will intrigue against me.'

'He cannot do that, if you come here and
conduct your oratorio in person.'

'But in the distribution of parts——

'Let us take counsel! You have the opportunity of hearing the best singers during the
time of your residence here, and you can
choose those whom you prefer, and write music
suitable for them. Never fear! Take special
pains with the choruses, which are admirably
effective here, and I wager you will be revenged
on the man and his evil-doings.'

I went to the opera every night, and, after
carefully noting in my pocket-book the compass
of voice and the style of each of the chief singers,

I take no great credit to myself for getting the best out of everyone, and for writing music specially adapted to each individual artist.

Immediately after my return to Silesia, Padre Pintus composed an oratorio for me, choosing the Biblical subject of Esther. I had finished my task within a month after I had the libretto; the parts were copied for my choir, and we had a few rehearsals of the work at Johannisberg. As I could not trust my own insight, for fear of self-complacency, I invited competent critics from Breslau and the neighbourhood, and even begged the musicians of the Prince's band to give me their real opinion freely and fearlessly, should they find fault with particular passages, here and there. I was determined to alter and polish the work, until every defect was removed, but neither I myself, nor any of the competent or incompetent critics, found any occasion to change a single note of the score.

Six weeks before the performance, I sent my original score to Vienna, promising to appear there before the concert.

The Prince showed great anxiety to hear the oratorio in Vienna, with an orchestra two hundred strong; but ever since the last treaty, he had been forbidden to appear in public, either at Court or at the Imperial headquarters, so he was afraid he would have to give up that pleasure. But when it was pointed out to him, that this veto was no bar to his appearing anywhere, in Vienna especially, if he went *incognito*, under another name and title,—and, further, that the Pope could travel as Bishop of Rome, parish priest, Dean, or Archbishop,—he saw the force of the comparison, and donning the ordinary short dress of a priest, he ventured to appear as Dean of Weidenau, a place in his diocese. He took me with him in his carriage, and was kind enough to pay my travelling expenses.

We arrived at Vienna at seven o'clock in the morning of the day agreed on, for we travelled day and night. At ten o'clock I visited Count Spork, who at once arranged that the first rehearsal should be in his own house. Three grand rehearsals were held in the theatre, on the following days. At my request, the Count was so polite as to forward the key of a box to the Dean of Weidenau, for all the rehearsals as well as for the two performances. This means a good deal in Vienna, where, as a rule, no one is permitted to be present, be he a noble or an ordinary person!

The Emperor Joseph came every time. Pichel told me, on the evening of my first rehearsal. which was held at noon, that His

Majesty had remarked, at one of his chamber concerts, ' Gaszmann wanted to put Ditters' nose out of joint, but Ditters has given his a regular twist ; for I much prefer his oratorio to Hasse's, and to Gaszmann's too.'

The first performance of my oratorio was on the last day of Advent, the second on the following Tuesday. I will merely state that, after the payment of all expenses, the Widows' Society profited to the tune of fourteen hundred and fifty florins—the proceeds after Gaszmann's oratorio having amounted only to five hundred and thirty.

I had been six weeks back in Johannisberg, when Pichel wrote to me that Gaszmann had died a fortnight before, and that the Emperor, contrary to all expectation, had announced that he was not going to fill up the place, though, as it carried a salary of three hundred ducats, there were many competitors. It appeared, therefore, that the Emperor was only waiting to see if I should come forward as a candidate, and I must make up my mind then and there.

I wrote back to say that I should not apply for the post, as I was making more money in Johannisberg, and I might hope to add to it ; but should the Emperor expressly desire me to stand, His Majesty might command me.

I really do not know whether Pichel was secretly commissioned to sound me, but I learnt afterwards that, when my answer was made known to the Emperor, he received it ungraciously.

'A dainty fellow, upon my word!' he is said to have exclaimed. 'Not only does he turn up his nose at a salary of three hundred ducats, but he wants me to go down on my knees to him. No, thank you!'

Bonno received the appointment, obviously to the Emperor's advantage, for Bonno had had a pension of eight hundred florins for many years. When this lapsed to the Treasury, the Emperor gave half the sum to Gaszmann's widow, and the other half to Salieri, whom he engaged to conduct his chamber music.

I come at last to the most important epoch of my life, that of my elevation to the nobility.

CHAPTER XXII.

I am promoted to the nobility, and become Amtshauptmann
—Lolli at Johannisberg—Anecdote of Quadagni, the
Venetian *castrato*.

In the year 1773 died Cajetan von Beeren-
berg, the Amtshauptmann of Freyenwaldau.
The Prince summoned me forthwith, and very
graciously offered me the vacant post.

'One thing is necessary,' he said. 'You
must be ennobled—else it will not do! A
fundamental law has prevailed in Breslau from
time immemorial, and no temporal Prince-
Bishop can depart from it—all the more that
such posts are, in a way, charitable foundations,
and a Prince-Bishop, who is obliged to keep great
state in Breslau, is thereby enabled to provide
for noblemen who are without means of their
own, his pages or his equerries, and so effectu
ally that not only are they themselves made in
dependent, but they are placed in such a position

as to give their children a proper education. In view of this fundamental law, none but a noble can receive the lucrative post of Amtshauptmann. If you can contrive to be raised to the nobility, the post will be given to you immediately. I only make one condition : that is, that you sign a bond obliging you to continue in my service during my lifetime, and never to quit it on any pretext whatever ; in return, you shall have my written assurance that, except with your consent, I will never dismiss you, nor abate the salary attached to your appointment. Now, apply to any clever agent in Vienna ; if the matter is settled, I will gladly contribute one-third of the usual expenses.'

Accordingly I made an application in Vienna, and received an assurance that the business should be settled without delay, if I could answer some questions affecting my family, my appointments, my revenues, and my moral character, to the satisfaction of the Court. These requisites were easily fulfilled ; so, within a short time, I not only received my diploma as Carl von Dittersdorf, but even before that, with the list of the fees, a flattering intimation that half of those due to the Court had been re-mitted, by especial favour of Maria Theresa. The whole affair cost no more than eleven hundred gulden, including the honorarium of fifty ducats for the agent, Herr von Hoffmann ; and the Prince, in accordance with his promise, contributed four hundred florins.

This altered name of mine has frequently led to all sorts of misunderstandings, particularly when direct orders from Paris were issued for many of my compositions.

Thus I was made Amtshauptmann of Freyen-waldau.   I was sworn in and received my diploma from the Cathedral Chapter, my formal installation taking place November 4, 1773 ; but as the Prince wished me to be with him constantly at Johannisberg, it was arranged that the Kammerrath should act as my deputy, and transact my business, receiving from me in return a considerable part of my salary.

Soon afterwards, Renner was made Schul-rektor of Johannisberg, with a salary of seven hundred florins, besides extra pay as a singer in the Prince's service ; these emoluments were, of course, for life.   My sister, too, was married to the Court Chancellor, von Gambsberg.

Our concerts and *spectacles* went on unin-terruptedly, and our orchestra was justly reckoned the best in all Imperial and Prussian Silesia.   The consequence was that many *virtuosi* on tour either wrote or came in person, asking to appear at the concerts. But I had been ordered by the Prince, once for all, to give a polite refusal to every applicant, telling him candidly, that the allowance for the band was so small as to admit of no extra outlay whatever. As the Prince disliked hearing any foreign artist without rewarding him, he was forced to give up that pleasure.

Sound and sensible musicians saw the reasonableness of this line of conduct, but the army of vagabonds decried me as a selfish man, who would not admit any stranger into the Prince's presence. I turned a deaf ear to such calumnies, and consoled myself with the consciousness of my duty.

Amongst these travelling *virtuosi* was a certain Rüsche, a good flute-player, who was insane enough to personate Vanhall, afterwards so popular as a composer. He came, in the character of Vanhall, to Johannisberg, but Vanhall having learnt from me, just as Pleyel had from Joseph Haydn, I knew for a certainty that, so far from being a skilled player, he had never put a flute to his lips. To be sure, I admitted the gentleman to an interview, but I rated him soundly for his impudence, and told him that, if he wanted to keep up the sham any longer, I would post his name in the public journals as a rascal and an impostor. So he went away crestfallen, but it may well be imagined that the courage of such a man revived when he got home, and that he held me up to execration. The faces of heroes are not more hopelessly disfigured in woodcuts than is the moral character of an honest man by many a vagabond rascal.

One day, the great *virtuoso*, Lolli, appeared at Johannisberg. He told me, as well as the Prince, who surprised him in my room, according to previous arrangement, that he had gone expressly six or seven miles out of his way from Freudenthal, not, as usual, in order to be heard, but to make my acquaintance, and to pay homage to the illustrious connoisseur. He was a tall, handsome fellow, a regular man of the world, and, with all his gifts, a modest, agreeable, and jovial companion. No wonder that the Prince soon became fond of him! He at once invited him to dinner, gave him a spare room in the Castle, and on the same evening ordered a performance of my opera 'Lo Sposo purlato' in his honour, the same work which, under the title of 'Der gefoppte Bräutigam,' was successfully performed at Brünn, Vienna, Grätz, Prague, Dresden, Weimar, and several places besides.

Lolli had only meant to stay for one day, but the Prince begged for another, and he graciously consented. We had hardly finished the symphony at our evening concert, when he asked the Prince's permission to be allowed to play a concerto, and a sonata as well, before the last symphony; his great reputation was amply confirmed by the performance. He was so delighted with his reception, that he kept on postponing the day of departure. For a whole fortnight, opera days excepted, we constantly enjoyed the display of his powers, and he spared no exertion to indemnify us for our politeness. His great knowledge of the world, and the charming manners that distinguished him most advantageously from so many other *virtuosi*, were enough to make me his friend at once.

Among the many anecdotes with which he often entertained us, two interested us more than the rest, and I should like to narrate one circumstantially, as it concerns his fortune in Venice, and the fright he experienced, on hearing that he was ordered for immediate execution. But as it would lead me too far out of the road, and its main features are already familiar enough,* I will turn to the other story

* The story is given, amongst others, in the first year of the *Allgemeine Musikalische Zeitung*, No. 39.

of the famous *castrato*, Quadagni of Venice—for the benefit of all bumptious *virtuosi*—for I have never yet come across that in my reading, and it deserves to be better known.

There was one opera—a special favourite with the Venetian public—in which Quadagni had appeared three times already, and shone conspicuously both as an actor and a singer. He had had some quarrel with the impresario, and, with the view of bringing about a complete *fiasco*, it occurred to him that he would turn the whole into ridicule, by seeming to forget his part. So, at the fourth repetition of the opera, he sang and acted worse than a schoolboy. The audience, thinking he was ill, let the matter pass; but the impresario took care that they should know the real cause of the breakdown. At the fifth performance Quadagni sang, if possible, still worse, but after the first act, two delegates came upon the stage, and, pointing out to him that the public, whom they represented, had nothing to do with his quarrels, they begged him to do his duty. He received the address with contemptuous laughter, and acted, if possible, worse in the second act. The deputation came again, with this message, that the audience *commanded* him to do his duty in the third act,

failing which, unexpected and unpleasant con-
sequences would ensue.

' I despise such threats,' answered the haughty
castrato. ' What I will not do of my own free
will, no power on earth shall compel me to do !'

He howled instead of singing ; he stood stock
still instead of acting.

Who would not have thought that the
audience would hunt him off the stage with
rotten apples and oranges, according to its
usual custom ? Contrary to all expectation
the performance went on quietly to the end.

When the opera was finished, and Quadagni
was about to get into his gondola, being still in
his actor's dress, over which he had thrown a
cloak, he was seized by four men in masks, who
bandaged his eyes, and hurried him off into
a boat. At last he found himself in a poorly
furnished but clean room, with a bed in it. Two
of the masked men remained with him. Some
time after, two others came in, carrying a table,
with a good supper on it. The hungry *castrato*, without more ado, sat down to eat, but one
of his custodians called out :

' Hands off, sir ! Unless you sing, not a
morsel shall you have.'

Quadagni refused. The mask ordered the
table to be sent away, and then went off.

This scene was repeated next day. Quadagni remained mute; the table and all the good things were shipped off again. So it went on for two whole days, but on the third day a perfectly irresistible soup was served up, and the fine gentleman, now at starvation-point, could hold out no longer.

'After all, I would rather sing than starve,' he exclaimed, and prepared to fall to.

'That is not enough, sir,' said the mask. 'If you do not sing—yes, and sing your *very best*— and *act* into the bargain, away goes the soup out of the door !'

What was to be done? Quadagni submitted and sang and acted as finely as if he were impelled by pure love of art.

' Bravo, bravissimo!' exclaimed all the masked critics, and clapped their hands vehemently.

The spokesman sat down by the side of the penitent, and the two enjoyed their supper together.

' Now, my good friend, let us see how things have come round!' said the mask, when the cloth was taken away. 'You insisted, first of all, that no force on earth should compel you, and now the public has gradually compelled you to sing, *without force*, and you cannot say otherwise. It is high time for you to learn who it is

before whom you have had the honour to perform, between these four unpretending walls.
For whom do you take me?'

Quadagni stood up deferentially, and said ·

'Perhaps *il Serenissimo Duca ?*'

'Your obedient servant, the executioner, at
your service!'

A peal of mocking laughter followed; the
distinguished company unmasked, and the
frightened *castrato*, seeing himself surrounded
by hangmen, sank to the ground with shame.

'The venerable Senate has, you see, allowed
the public this slight compensation for the
gross insult which you offered them. You are
now free from arrest! A gondola is already
before my door, and it shall take you home. I
am commissioned to warn you to do your duty
at all future performances. If you do not,
you may be sure that the Senate will treat a
second insult far more seriously.'

After this epilogue Quadagni returned home,
a sadder, wiser man, and from that hour he
behaved more decently and modestly, which is
saying a good deal for a *castrato*. He sang
again; he sang and acted with redoubled
energy. The public made its peace with him,
and he was reinstalled as a favourite.

But what became of Lolli, whom we have

left all this time at Johannisberg? He took leave of us after a fortnight. Seven months elapsed, and he wrote from St. Petersburg to say that he was engaged at a salary of four thousand roubles. After three years, the Czarina gave him a year's leave to travel. He came by way of Neisse to Johannisberg, on purpose to pay his respects to the Prince once more; he was in such a hurry that he wanted to be off next day—and yet he stayed five full days with us! He confessed to me that he had no wish to return to Russia, and that, with the view of obtaining a formal and honourable discharge from the Empress, he had commissioned a well-known physician to draw up a certificate, to the effect that the Russian climate was dangerous to his weak chest, and would certainly bring him prematurely to the grave. This is a refutation of the story in the *Allgemeine Musikalische Zeitung*, that, in dudgeon at the Czarina's command to Giardini to play the adagios* in his concertos and solos, he had asked to resign, and had thereupon been sent off to Siberia.

* 'The Abbé Bertini plainly states that Lolli . . . was unable to play an adagio properly. . . . "I am a native of Bergamo," he said; "we are all born fools at Bergamo—how should I play a serious piece?"'—See 'The Dictionary of Music,' article 'Lolli.'

I must once again do him the justice to say that, if rather haughty in dealing with great people, he was a polite, modest, and agreeable man. Unlike most of his compatriots, he wore his heart upon his sleeve. By his own confession, he had formerly an irresistible passion for games of chance, for he assured me that he had gambled away more than three-fourths of his property. Now, however, he was quite free from it. He actually showed me, in private, bank-notes and cash to the value of about ten thousand gulden. He was going to make a tour through Vienna, Paris, London, Amsterdam, Hamburg, Berlin, and the Papal States, and then he meant to try and keep whatever he gained, to lodge it safely in a Government bank, and to live quietly on the interest. But what became of it, and where he is now, I do not know.

CHAPTER XXIII.

The Johannisberg band is dismissed—The Amtshauptmann
in a dilemma—The snare from which I escaped.

THE Prince dismissed his band, in consequence
of the outbreak of the War of the Bavarian
Succession, and the hostilities between Austria
and Prussia, but he assured the musicians that,
in the event of peace and the restoration of his
revenues, he would take back again every one
of them.

Having nothing more to do with the orchestra,
I retired with my family to Freyenwaldau, where
I fulfilled my duties, as Amtshauptmann, as
strictly and conscientiously as I could. The
Prince, meantime, withdrew to Brünn—for he
was too near the enemy's territory to feel
secure—and the result showed that he was wise.
General Kirchheim was under orders from the
Austrians to guard the principality of Neisse on-
this-side from the Prussians, but his army of

three thousand men failed to prevent them from taking Johannisberg, and making themselves masters of the larger half, as far as the mountain range of Freyenwaldau and Zuckmantel. It was impossible to dislodge them from Johannisberg, for they had the protection of the Glatz behind them.

I had not much anxiety on the score of a hostile attack upon Freyenwaldau, for General Lövenöhr, who guarded the position, had plenty of men, though it was always possible, if the armies of Prince Henry and the King advanced into Bohemia, that the Prussians might push in from that side, by way of Troppau, in which case the Zuckmantel outposts would be forced to retire from our neighbourhood, in order to avoid being completely cut off. But I had many reasons for regretting that I had settled down with the Prince-Bishop, instead of going about the world and trying my luck, and that I was tied to an official post, the duties of which in war-time involved so much responsibility, discomfort, and uneasiness. It is no joke for a high official to have an army—even if it is not a large army—quartered on him in his particular province. He is surrounded by thousands of petty anxieties. Baggage and transport must be looked after, and, worst of all, there is the incessant danger of the enemy attacking at any moment. One slight instance will suffice to show on what footing I stood, with regard to the enemy, when things were in this unfortunate position.

Before the outbreak of hostilities, the Prince was permitted by the Imperial Court to sell to Tasso, the Prussian merchant of Neisse, eight thousand piles of cord-wood, on the understanding that this quantity of fuel should be floated to Neisse, in the early spring, at the purchaser's cost. The war had just begun, when a special messenger was despatched to the Prince, with a royal order, forbidding the embarkation of the eight thousand piles, and threatening an embargo. Meantime, General Stutterheim, in command of the third army of the enemy, had taken Troppau, and the purchaser of the wood, who was with me at Freyenwald, where the cargo was, brought me the money, and wanted to put the timber on the river. But I produced the prohibition from the Court, and absolutely refused to let the consignment go. He rushed off to Troppau in despair, and, after applying to General Stutterheim, returned to me in the course of a week, with the following order :

' After reading this order, Herr von Dittersdorf, the Amtshauptmann of Freyenwaldau, is commanded to allow the transport of the eight thousand piles of timber to Neisse, the timber having been already negotiated for by the merchant Tasso. In event of non-compliance with the order, I am empowered to enforce it with fire and sword.

'VON STUTTERHEIM.'

But I was not to be scared. I kept this order to myself, and, after positively refusing to float the cargo, I sent the bearer of the message back just as he came. At the same time, I told the Landeshauptmann, who, with his family, had sought refuge in Freyenwaldau, what I had done.

'What are your intentions?' said he.

'I mean to send a copy of the order to the General in command of our outposts, and the original to Duke Albert, who is Inspector of the Moravian Armies, notifying my refusal to both, but asking at the same time for sufficient protection.'

'Good!' said he. 'Those are my views too.'

I undertook to draw up both reports, and the whole thing was settled in two hours. The Landeshauptmann had to sign also. We sent one by courier to the Duke's headquarters, which were between Moravia and Bohemia, but the other was forwarded by military escort to the Commandant. A week elapsed, and we received His Royal Highness's reply, in which he graciously praised our conduct, and promised us assistance. Another week passed, and we were reinforced by a regiment of Infantry, five squadrons of Hussars, a Dragoon regiment, three Volunteer battalions, and two of Croats. The order strictly forbade us to give the slightest ground for any suspicion of partiality towards the enemy, adding that every Imperial officer who came near us would be instructed to watch us narrowly, and at once to report to the authorities anything which seemed likely to tell against us. Though conscious that we could not be charged with the slightest dereliction of duty, it was very disagreeable to feel that every officer was commissioned to play the part of a detective towards us.

Besides this, traps were laid for me, now here, now there, into which the enemy would certainly have enticed me, had I been silly enough. I will only give one instance.

A senior Lieutenant, von Scholten by name, a Prussian, had occupied the Castle at Johannisberg with a battalion. He had some cannon and a few howitzers with him. After fortifying

Johannisberg to the teeth, he seized the Prince's revenues, set fire to towns and villages, parsonages and convents, and took up a strong position, protected as he was by the Glatz Mountains. Having five more battalions of infantry and ten squadrons of cavalry at his disposition in the neighbouring country, he made several efforts to force his way to Freyenwaldau, in order to get possession of the mountain range also. But the two passes of Setzdorf and Sandhübel were so well fortified by Nature that a small force could defend them, so he was always compelled to retire. What he would have liked to do was, to levy a contribution from the whole province of Freyenwaldau, in which there was a little town and twenty-seven villages; but that being impossible, except by force of arms, he had recourse to a stratagem, which, to be candid, was silly enough.

I received an autograph letter, conveyed by the Amtsdiener of Johannisberg, who was allowed by him to go to and fro between us. It was as follows:

‘ Being a devoted lover of music, I am longing to make the personal acquaintance of a man whose great musical gifts I have held in honour for many years. I invite you to take pot-luck here to-morrow in Johannisberg, that I may have this great delight. Awaiting you with open arms,

> 'Your most obedient servant
> 'VON SCHOLTEN,
> 'Senior Lieutenant of the Royal Prussian Army.'

After reading this document, I sent a verbal answer through the official :

'If you are ever so bold as to bring me such a message from the enemy again, I shall fold it the wrong way, and send it to the Imperial head-quarters. You may tell the Senior Lieutenant Scholten, that I have no wish to surrender myself as a hostage into the enemy's hands, merely for the sake of pot-luck and of being received by him with open arms. Be off with you!

I enclosed the note in the report which I drew up of the transaction, and the General replied by sending me an agreeable letter of commendation.

Our blockade lasted to the time of the conclusion of peace, and every fortnight, as a rule, the Imperial forces were on the alert, on the two passes, as well as in Zuckmantel itself. But it was soon discovered that this was done only to give employment to the Imperial corps in covering the pass, and hindering them from attacking the Prussian transports, which had to go within two miles of Zuckmantel, every fortnight. It ended at last in the endeavour of General Wunsch to attack the Lövenör corps in Zuckmantel with twenty thousand men, with the view, if not of defeating or annihilating, at least of dislodging them from the mountain recesses. Swift and determined as his onset was, nothing came of it, and that because of an accident, which led to a blunder on the part of a General who had already acquired fame and experience in the Seven Years' War. But the whole story is too long to be told here.

CHAPTER XXIV.

The Johannisberg band is reinstated—Ovid's 'Metamorphoses'—My interview with the Emperor Joseph—Hofkapellmeister Greybig—Origin of my German operas.

AFTER the Treaty of Peace concluded at Teschen, the Prince remained some time longer at Brünn, that he might see to the restoration of the Castle, which had been almost demolished by the enemy. After his return to Johannisberg, he at once readmitted to his service some members of the Court band, whom he had dismissed before the war broke out, and who now presented themselves again. New members were substituted for the rest, and the orchestra and chorus were entirely re-modelled by the time the winter began. The Prince was not able to afford a theatre, for the restoration of his property, which had been ruined by the enemy, demanded a large outlay.

I still lived on in Freyenwaldau, but the Prince was always asking for me, and I was often detained a week or a fortnight at Johannisberg. In short, I had become indispensable to him. My official duties suffered from my repeated absence, so once again I was allowed a deputy, and returned to Johannisberg, where I bought a place, built a house, and planned a beautiful garden. This outlay not only emptied my pockets of ready cash, but involved me in a burden of debt, to the amount of near upon five thousand gulden.

Years before this time, I had been petitioned by the Society for the Widows of Musicians at Vienna, to write another oratorio for their benefit. To this at last I assented, and at the end of Lent, 1786, I conducted my oratorio 'Giobbe,' or 'Hiob,' at Vienna. The papers were loud in my praises, but it does not become me to say more than that the two first performances of the Society brought in something like a clear profit of seventeen hundred gulden.

On this occasion I came across *seven* foreign violinists, who were all there on speculation, and came together quite unexpectedly. Foremost among them were Jarnowich, Frenzel *père*, and a certain S., who belonged to the

German Empire. The superiority of S. consisted in double-stopping and arpeggios, which he paraded *ad nauseam*. Every moment he was making some clumsy transition, or running counter to the rules of true composition, so that every real connoisseur had his teeth set on edge.

Three years before, it had occurred to me to take some of Ovid's 'Metamorphoses' as subjects for characteristic symphonies, and by the time of my arrival in Vienna, I had already finished twelve of them. By way of compensating myself for my travelling expenses, I ventured on a speculation with this music of mine, which was attended with such remarkable incidents that I must make rather a long story of it.

By special permission of the Emperor Joseph, which I had obtained with the help of a certain Herr von Bourguignon, I had advertised six symphonies in the great *Saal* of the Imperial Augarten (tickets two gulden each), and Baron van Swieten himself had undertaken to distribute a hundred of them. But the weather was very bad about that time, and threatened to continue bad, so my subscribers begged me to postpone the performance until we had a change. I went to the Police Office, and asked

for leave to call in my public announcements, as
well as to alter the day of performance; but
they told me that this necessitated a new order
from the Cabinet, which, however, if I really
wanted it, might be got that very day.

'After the Court is over,' said the President,
'go at once to the so-called Controller's lobby!
The middle door there leads to the entrance of
the Emperor's private Chancery Office. You
will find some of his body-servants in a small
room on the right-hand side. Ask one of them
for Herr von Bourguignon; he will get you
permission, and perhaps the Emperor himself
will speak to you.'

'So much the better!' said I, and went off in
all haste to the Court.

Conscious that anyone admitted to the
Emperor's presence must speak shortly, clearly,
boldly, and without cringing, I determined to
follow that rule. The lackey announced me
to Herr von Bourguignon, but instead of him
the Emperor himself appeared, and the following
dialogue began between us.

The Emperor: 'Hulloa! what do you want
with me?'

I: 'I want nothing of Your Majesty.'

Emperor: 'What do you mean?'

I: 'My business is too trifling for Your

Majesty to be troubled with it.   I only wanted an interview with Herr von Bourguignon.'

Emperor (jocosely) : 'Well, if it's no secret, I will tell the gentleman.'

I (in the same tone): 'Oh, that is not necessary!   Your Majesty can decide the matter yourself, and I would rather you did so.'

Emperor (as before) : 'Come in!'   (He took me into a small room adjoining the secret Chancery.)   'Well, what is it all about?'

I· 'The President of the Police has sent me here.'

Emperor (still jocosely) : 'Oh, oh! the President of the Police!   Have you been plotting?   Have you got into the claws of the Commissioner of Modesty?'

I (in the same tone) : 'Oh, the police would have assigned me some little place already, and I should not now be having the honour——'

Emperor : 'Come, let the cat out of the bag!'

I : 'My subscribers want me to postpone my music in the Augarten, because of the bad weather.   The Head of the Police cannot give me permission without the leave of the Court, and for that reason I am here.'

Emperor (advancing to the door of the private Chancery) : 'Bourguignon, do you hear me ? Write a short note to the President of the Police, and say I allow Dittersdorf to postpone his music in the Augarten for as long as he likes.' (To me :) ' By-the-bye, I have been uncommonly pleased with your oratorio " Hiob," and have had a copy of the score made for myself. I hope you have no objection ?'

I : ' I am only too delighted to have earned the praise of so great a connoisseur as You Majesty.'

Emperor (coldly) · ' I hate flattery. The truth for me, and nothing but the truth !'

I : ' So much the better, for I have spoken the truth.'

Emperor (after a short pause) : ' Have you heard the foreign *virtuosi* on the violin ?'

I : ' I have heard seven of them.'

Emperor : ' As you yourself are a first-rate player——'

I : ' I was once, but am now no more.'

Emperor : ' Why not ?'

I : ' Because I have given up playing for many years past.'

Emperor · ' It is just the same ; anyhow, you are still *judex competens*. Who is the best amongst the seven ?'

I (shrugging my shoulders) : ' I had rather

not praise one at the expense of the others so let me say that each has his good points.'

Emperor: 'The usual modesty of you *virtuosi!* I want to know for certain which you think the best of the lot.'

I: 'Jarnowich.'

Emperor: 'Well, what are his good points?'

I: 'He has a fine tone, and plays his scales clearly. He misses no notes in his allegro, sings admirably in his adagio,—here and there he has his *minauderies.*'

Emperor: 'But he is not such a trickster as Lolli.'

I: 'And, best of all, he plays with freedom —no grimaces ; in a word, he plays for the art and for the heart.'

Emperor: 'He plays, I suppose, just as Dittersdorf once played? Well, I am glad you agree with me! What think you of S. ? Tell me candidly.'

I: 'If Your Majesty expressly orders me to say what I think, I must say that he tires and bores me to death with his everlasting double-stoppings and arpeggios.'

Emperor: '*Bravissimo!* I say the same ; yet Greybig is ready to go to the stake for him, and we are perpetually quarrelling about it. But to-day I will shut his mouth by telling him that I made you the umpire, and that you have decided in my favour. I shall have the laugh of him.'

I (quietly entering into the spirit of the joke) : ' Heaven forbid ! Your Majesty will get me into hot water with Greybig, and I had far rather be in his good books.'

Emperor (laughing) : ' Surely you are not afraid of that Jack-pudding !'

I : ' Oh, but I am ! For when he hears that I disagree with him, he will praise me in a much nastier fashion than he praised Haydn and Mozart.'

Emperor : ' Your sentence was pronounced long ago.'

I : ' Alas for me !'

Emperor : ' It is not so bad as you fear. Would you like to hear it ?'

I : ' I am all attention.'

Emperor : ' He says that as a violinist you are like a good preacher, who, however, shows himself better read in the Old than in the New Testament.'

I : ' Satirical enough.'

Emperor · ' But he says of your composition that it is a well-furnished, daintily-arranged table The dishes are well served up. One can take a good helping from each, without risk to the digestion. I heartily agree with **Greybig** in his criticism of your composition.'

I: 'Your Majesty is too kind.'

Emperor: 'There is nothing kind in doing a man justice. Do you still hold your appointment in Silesia?'

I: 'Yes, Your Majesty.'

Emperor: 'As what?'

I: 'As Amtshauptmann and **Regierungsrath.**'

Emperor: 'What sort of business have you to look after?'

I: '*Publica, Politica et Judicialia.*'

Emperor (earnestly): 'Indeed! Are you properly qualified?'

I: 'I have already held the post for thirteen years, and have never yet been criticised.'

Emperor: 'I am glad to hear it. But where on earth did you get the knowledge requisite for such duties?'

I: 'I should be eternally disgraced if I, who was born and brought up in Vienna, had learnt nothing else but violin-playing and composition.'

Emperor (still more gravely): 'H'm! Your answers are direct enough.'

I (in a tone of deep respect): 'I have been taught that Your Majesty expects short, concise, and unvarnished answers. If I am mistaken, I ask your pardon.'

Emperor (more gently) : 'You have been taught correctly, and your answers have not offended me.' (Then, after a short pause, and with his former air of condescension :) ' Have you heard Mozart play ?'

I : ' Three times already.'

Emperor : ' Do you like him ?'

I : ' Yes ; all musicians do.'

Emperor : ' You have heard Clementi too ?'

I : ' Yes.'

Emperor · ' Some prefer him to Mozart, and Greybig is at the head of them. What do you think ? Out with it !'

I : 'Clementi's playing is art simply and solely ; Mozart's combines art and taste.'

Emperor : ' I say the same. You and I seem to have taken a leaf out of the same book.'

I : ' That we have ; and, what is more, out of that great book—*experience.*'

Emperor · ' What do you think of Mozart's compositions ?'

I : ' He is unquestionably one of the greatest original geniuses, and I have never yet met with any composer who had such an amazing wealth of ideas ; I could almost wish he were not so lavish in using them. He leaves his hearer out of breath ; for hardly has he grasped one beautiful thought, when another of greater fascination dispels the first, and this goes on throughout, so that in the end it is impossible to retain any one of these beautiful melodies.'

Emperor : ' He has one only fault in his pieces for the stage, and his singers have very often complained of it—he deafens them with his full accompaniment.'

I : ' That surprises me !   One can introduce and blend harmony and the play of accompaniment, without spoiling the *cantilena.*'

Emperor : ' You have this gift in perfection. I have observed it in your two oratorios, " Esther " and " Hiob."   What do you think of Haydn's compositions ?'

I : ' I have not heard any of his dramatic pieces.'

Emperor : ' You lose nothing in that, for he writes exactly as Mozart does.   But what do you think of his chamber music ?'

I : ' Why, it is making a world-wide sensation, and most justly too.'

Emperor : ' Is he not often too playful ?'

I : ' He has the gift of sportiveness. but he never loses the dignity of art.'

Emperor · ' You are right there.'   (After a pause :) ' Some time ago, I drew a parallel be-

tween Mozart and Haydn; I wish you would
do the same, that I may see whether you agree
with me.'

I (after a pause) : ' Before I do so, will Your
Majesty allow me to ask you a question ?'

Emperor : ' Certainly.'

I : 'What think you of a parallel between
Klopstock and Gellert ?'

Emperor · ' H'm ! They are both great
poets. To understand all his beauty, one must
read Klopstock's works over and over again,
whereas Gellert's merits are patent at the first
glance.'

I : ' Here Your Majesty has my answer.'

Emperor · ' Mozart, then, may be compared
with Klopstock, and Haydn with Gellert ?'

I : ' That is my opinion, anyhow.'

Emperor : ' Charming ! Now you have once
more put a rod into my hand, and I shall beat
that goose, Greybig, with it.'

I · ' May I be so bold as to ask Your Majesty
about your parallel ?'

Emperor · ' You may. I compared Mozart's
compositions to a gold snuff-box, manufactured
in Paris, and Haydn's to one finished off in
London.' (Advancing to the Chancery door :)
' Have you done, Bourguignon?' (B. brought
him a note, whereupon he said to me :) ' I

am glad to be better acquainted with you; I find you are quite a different man from what they told me.'

I : 'In what respect, Your Majesty?'

Emperor · ' They told me you were an egotist, who grudged the smallest recognition to any *virtuoso,* or to any other composer. That was what made me try your sensitive point, and I am glad that I found just the contrary. I will make certain folk smart for this! One, to be sure, has gone long ago *ad patres.*' (He gave me the note.) ' Here is my permission for the performance of your music in the Augarten, whenever you like. Adieu!'

He went into the private Chancery, and I to the Police Office.

Greybig's name appears in this dialogue. He, with his ridiculous airs of self-importance, was an occasional source of amusement to the Emperor. I will tell one story about him, that he may be the better appreciated by my readers.

One evening the Emperor went to the Marinelli Theatre in the Leopoldstadt. Kasperl, as the Night Watch, sang an air in his best comic style, and the Emperor, who had a good bass voice, was so delighted that he ordered the song to be copied, and sang it at his own private concert. He often repeated the performance, introducing by degrees all Kasperl's jokes and his by-play.

'Well, what do you think of it?' he once asked Greybig. 'Do I sing the aria as Kasperl does?'

'Oh, oh, oh!' replied Greybig, with his usual happy inspiration, 'upon my soul, Your Majesty *is Kasperl to the life !*'

The Emperor cried with laughter.

'My dear Greybig.' said he at last, 'you have put your foot into it! To call me a Jack-pudding* in the face of my own orchestra!'

'Eh, eh, eh!' replied Greybig. 'I did not mean that; it escaped me without my knowing. I ask your pardon.'

'Oh,' answered the Emperor, 'you are forgiven long ago! Of course you know that one cannot be angry with *certain people.*'

'I suppose you mean fools?'

'That is it,' replied the Emperor. 'Meanwhile, you have taken ample revenge on me for often calling you a noodle. However, that does not matter ! The difference is, that I was a Jack-pudding only so long as I was singing, but you will be a noodle now and ever, *per omnia sæcula sæculorum.*'

As soon as the weather cleared up, I gave

* *Kasperl* is the German for Jack-pudding.

my first six Ovidian symphonies in the Augarten;
the others a week later, at the theatre. After
deducting some important items, besides the
copying of the parts, I had to pay an orchestra
of forty persons, and even then I cleared three
times as much as my journeys to and fro had
cost me. I was just about to pack up mv
traps, when the actor, Stephani the younger,
who was also overseer of German opera, paid
me a visit, having been commissioned by the
directors to ask me to write an opera in German,
on the usual terms of a hundred ducats. I consented. Herr Stephani provided the libretto,
and in six months' time the 'Doktor und
Apotheker' was performed. Complying with
the repeated request of the directors, I wrote
two more operas in German and one in
Italian, all in the space of *seven* months.
The three first, 'Doktor und Apotheker,'
'Betrug durch Aberglauben,' and 'Die Liebe
im Narrenhause' went *alle stelle*, as the Italians
say; but the Italian opera, 'Democrito,' was a
failure.

Before setting out on my return journey to
Silesia, in February, 1787, I went off to the
Emperor, to thank him for the money I had
made by my four operas. We had the same
sort of conversation as before, only on this

occasion he asked me what I thought of the Italian operas that I had heard in Vienna ? I gave him my candid opinion, praising what I liked, blaming what I disliked.

' I rather pique myself on my connoisseur-ship of music,' he said, ' because my judgment invariably coincides with yours. When do you intend to set off ?'

I : ' The day after to-morrow.'

Emperor (after walking up and down the room, reflectively) : 'Cannot you put off your journey for a week ?'

I : ' If Your Majesty pleases.'

Emperor : ' Good! I wish you would do so. Now, listen! I will order your " Apotheker " to be repeated next Saturday, and I think that our people here would be gratified if you would conduct your own opera in person, and allow us to advertise the fact that you intend to direct the work yet once more, for the very last time, in honour of your final leave-taking of the public.'

I · ' If Your Majesty pleases.'

Emperor · 'Well, that is settled! I myself will be present, so we shall meet once more. Farewell until then !'

I made all the arrangements, and my opera was performed. Next day, Herr von Horwath, the Treasurer, handed me two hundred ducats,

17

on behalf of the Emperor, His Majesty having graciously presented me with the entire receipts of the performance. By the advice of that official, I hurried off at once, so as to thank him before he went to Mass. Again he received me graciously, talking to me for more than half an hour, paid me many compliments on my style, whether grave or humorous, and finally dismissed me, with the words ·

' Come to Vienna as often as you please, and whenever your business will let you ! Be sure to come and see me ; it will always be a pleasure, particularly as we sympathize entirely in our views about music.'

CHAPTER XXV.

Gloomy prospects at Johannisberg—*Premonitory symptoms of gout*—My conversation with King Friedrich Wilhelm at Breslau.

ON my return to Johannisberg, I paid off a number of my debts with the money I had earned in Vienna. I found great alterations at Court. It was intended to separate the episcopal property under the Emperor's jurisdiction from the bishopric on the further side, and to draw from it a fund for religious purposes, after the death of the Prince-Bishop; but to prevent any deterioration during the lifetime of the Prince, Baron Kaschnitz, Steward of the Moravian estates of the Emperor, was entrusted with the administration. When he took office, as far back as 1785, he put aside fourteen thousand florins annually for the Prince, but from that sum were deducted ecclesiastical and other dues. The Prince's servants had to take the oath to the Emperor, and their incomes were pretty closely docked. I lost considerably; I used to draw two thousand seven hundred florins, and was now reduced to eighteen hundred.

During my residence in Vienna, the Prince fell out with the Administration, and complained to the Court; but it was his fate, that such injustice as cried to Heaven—well, I will keep my thoughts on these matters to myself! Enough; the result was that, in lieu of his former allowance of fourteen thousand florins (what an unheard-of falling off!), he now received only four thousand. I refrain from making any remark. It is too bitter a subject; this is what happens if you—— But silence!

Friedrich II. died soon after this decree, which was so fatal to the Prince. He wrote to his successor, Friedrich Wilhelm, petitioning to be reappointed to the bishopric of Breslau. The new King was well disposed, and forwarded the Prince's petition to the Chamber of Breslau, with a proposal to arrange matters as best they could. The Chamber answered, most submissively, that, although there was no difficulty about the reappointment in itself, all the Bishop's revenues, up to the present time, had been turned into a fund, to meet the exigencies of the State. Would His Majesty therefore graciously order the assignation of another fund? It was plain that the Chamber of Breslau shrank from giving up the administration of the estates—it is easy to guess why—and the object of its wishes was thus attained. The royal answer was framed in these words:

The restoration of the Prince-Bishop to the royal Prussian estates is impossible; but in order not to deprive him of all consolation, the King will allow him as much money a year, from the episcopal estates sequestrated in Prussian Silesia, as he shall be proved to have drawn from the property, in former days, under the Emperor's jurisdiction.'

Now, these revenues, as was well known in Prussia, without any further proof, did not amount to more than four thousand florins, so that a precisely similar sum was decreed from this quarter, the consequence being that the Prince's yearly revenues *in omni et toto* amounted to eight thousand gulden! My excellent master was so hard pressed that he had to economize, and some of the better-paid members of the orchestra were dismissed.

Meantime, the existing band and chorus had led to the education of a number of amateurs of both sexes. Foremost among the ladies

was Freyin von Zedlitz, the daughter of
the late Landeshauptmann, besides the two
Baronesses von Tauber, who, like their friend,
had become first-rate singers. Many old
members of the band had accepted civic em-
ployments, and remained on as officials. To
these must be added two more—Regierungs-
räthe von Böhm and Richter. They were
useful in the orchestra. Many of the sons
and daughters of the citizens joined in the
chorus. As one and all played and sang for
nothing, in order to please the sensitive Prince,
we were, thus constituted, a fairly creditable
body. I never slackened my labours until we
had a little theatre again ; this, however, was
not erected in the Castle, but in the suburbs,
where the shooting took place. The Prince
still had some spare cash in his privy purse,
and he subscribed a few hundred gulden to
the building.

But how were we to find an occasion for
keeping up our dramas ? It occurred to me to
have a paying performance for the benefit of
the Charitable Institute of the town, and of the
diocese generally. So, at the entrance door of
the box-office we posted the ' Oberkapelan,' as
chief guardian of the poor, a magistrate, and
two Poor Law guardians, who were substantial

citizens. After payment of all expenses, the Institution was still a considerable gainer; for, after the first public annual audit, not only were all debts cleared, but there was a surplus profit of from four to five hundred gulden. During this epoch, I compiled many more operas, besides those three, in German, which had been performed at Vienna. Many of these have been given at different theatres in Germany.

Now came on the premonitory symptoms of a misfortune, which has cruelly persecuted me ever since.

From time to time I was attacked by pains in my feet, and Stolle, the Prince's body-physician, pronounced these to be signs of gout. This was the cause of it.

Late in the autumn of 1788, Prince Hohenlohe, General of Infantry and acting Governor of Breslau, sent me an express to say that the King meant to sup with him after the review, and that he had to get up a concert for His Majesty's amusement. Would I come to Breslau, on receipt of this message, and under-take the arrangements? Ill as I was, I set out that same evening, travelled all night, and arrived at Breslau at ten in the morning. Rain and a cold north wind had damaged me to the extent of bringing on acute pains in my left foot.   However, I made very little of it, and after announcing my arrival, I was at once asked to join the Prince at dinner.   We talked over the programme.   The King arrived two days afterwards, and the concert was given on the same evening.

Hardly was the first symphony over, when the King came up and addressed me.

' I am deeply indebted to Prince Hohenlohe for having so agreeably surprised me by your presence.   I am glad to hear you again, after so many years.'

' Pardon me, Your Majesty!' I answered. 'I have given up solos for the last eight years.'

' Oh,' said the King, ' I hope you will play, to please me!'

I did so, and the King was good enough to say that ten years ago I could not have played better.   Then he asked for my four new symphonies, and after saying many pretty things about my compositions, he nodded in a friendly way, and withdrew.   Next day, at three o'clock, I was summoned.

Thank you for the pleasure you gave me yesterday,' said he, 'and also for the four symphonies, which the Prince has presented to me in your name.'

I : ' I hope that they will be more effective, when played by Your Majesty's orchestra.'

King : ' My band is pretty good.'

I : ' So I have heard.'

King : ' I wish you would pay me a visit in Berlin, and convince yourself of the fact.'

I : ' Next year I shall have the honour of paying my respects to Your Majesty.'

King · ' You have written some bright, merry music in your " Apotheker." I have often heard it with pleasure in Berlin.'

I : It is my first effort in that *genre.*'

King : ' But where do you get all your new ideas from ?'

I : ' If I am so fortunate as to have them occasionally, they come of themselves. Unless they come spontaneously, the game is up.'

King : ' That seems to be the case with K.'

I : ' Perhaps he has over - written himself, and exhausted his fancy ?'

King · ' Not exactly that. There is a sort of *stérilité* about his things, and yet he has no greater admirer than himself.'

I · ' What a glorious prospect for music, that another great King should have arisen, who so well understands it !'

King : ' Understands it ! No, I will not say that ; but I am very fond of it.'

Everyone knows that King Friedrich Wilhelm enjoyed talking about music. By dint of various questions and answers, I succeeded in making him more communicative than ever, and I took the opportunity of telling a story or two, *à propos* of the subject, rather humorously. The King laughed heartily time after time, and I was with him for more than an hour and a half. At last he dismissed me, graciously reminding me of my promise to come to Berlin.

I met Rietz, the Controller of the Privy Purse, in the ante-chamber.

'You have stayed a long while with His Majesty,' said he, 'and you have scared away his bad temper for to-day.'

'Bad temper?' I asked.

'The King was very cross at the review,' he continued, 'and he put some of the staff officers under arrest. That sort of thing generally lasts the whole day ; but judging from the laughter I heard just now, you have given us back our good King again, for whenever he laughs, all is forgotten.'

He ended by saying that the King had commissioned him to give me a little souvenir, in return for the pleasure he had enjoyed yesterday, and for my symphonies. It was a beautiful diamond ring of *aqua prima*, value three hundred ducats.

'Oh!' said I, 'pray be so good as to let me have one more interview with His Majesty, that I may thank him in person for his valuable present.'

'It was to spare you this trouble, that the King sent it *through me*, but I will do what you wish in the matter.'

After the King's departure, I remained some days longer in Breslau, being hospitably entertained by Prince Hohenlohe and other friends; I never had a moment to myself. But this luxurious life day by day, coming upon a chill which I had caught on my journey, brought about a fulfilment of Dr. Stolle's prophecy, earlier than either he or I had anticipated. On the fourth day, I was seized with an unmistakable fit of gout, and at Breslau I had to take to my bed. For nine days I endured tortures which are only known to adepts in that peculiarly malignant disease, and are incredible to every other. I had let myself be dragged to Johannisberg in an invalid carriage like a hearse, and on arriving, I was forced to take to my bed again, and to languish there for five weeks. For a long while I had to depend upon crutches, before I recovered the use of my feet again.

During that winter, I made preparations for my journey to Berlin, and I composed six new symphonies. On hearing that the Hereditary Statthalterin of Holland, the King's sister, was coming to Berlin towards the end of July, and that a whole month was to be given up to festivities in her honour, I chose to go at that favourable moment.

CHAPTER XXVI.

My journey to Berlin—Reichardt—*Professor Engel*—I am
introduced by the King to the Queen—My oratorio,
'Hiob,' is performed at the Grand Opera-house—The
operas 'Medea' and 'Protesilao'—Madame Rietz—
Disputes at the theatre—My wishes are more than
realized.

I TOOK my eldest son with me to Berlin. He
was a lad of fifteen at that time, with considerable gifts for composition. My object was
partly to introduce him to the great world,
partly to give him the chance of hearing
foreign musicians, and seeing good operas and
plays.

The King had gone to the border, to meet
his sister, and the Court was just then at Potsdam. I was advised to write to His Majesty,
asking for instructions whether or no to come
there ; but I was told that I might stay on in
Berlin, and he would give me an interview as
soon as he arrived.

During that time, I had been introduced by Herr Lippert to Herr Reichardt, the Royal Kapellmeister. Lippert had formerly acted the part of Sichel in my 'Apotheker' at Vienna, and now we met again here. He was agreeably surprised by my calling on him, and he treated me with the greatest courtesy and kindness, offering at the same time to introduce me to various friends. He took me that same evening to Struensee, the present Minister, who not only invited me to sup with him then, but did me the honour of asking me to dinner or supper perhaps more than ten times whilst I was in Berlin.

Reichardt had set to music Goethe's 'Claudine von Villa Bella,' for the coming Festival. I attended a rehearsal forthwith, thanks to the kindness of Professor Engel, who shared with Rammler the directorship of the German Theatre. The music was truly charming. Engel sat by my side in the pit at the rehearsal, and we had the following conversation, which is, I think, not without interest ·

Engel: ' I suppose you know this piece ?'

I: ' Reichardt sent it to me only yesterday, and I have just read it through.'

E.: ' I hope you will take the trouble to write music for it.'

I : ' That I will never do.'

E. · ' Why not ?'

I : ' For several reasons.'

E. : ' Indeed ! Will you not have the goodness to explain yourself more clearly ?'

I : ' I will give you one reason, but the others I keep *in petto.* I dislike borrowing a subject from another man, especially so famous a man as Herr Reichardt. Such musical tournaments are not to my taste, and I have no sort of wish to unhorse any composer, be he who he may.'

E. : ' I like your modesty, but obviously the public is the loser thereby.'

I : ' Not by this piece, for I can see beforehand that, if I were to set it, it would not be popular ; and I am truly sorry for all the trouble Herr Reichardt has bestowed upon it, and for the loss of his glorious music.'

E. : ' Perhaps the orchestra is to blame ?'

I : ' No, no !—far from it. Every man there is up to the mark.'

E. : ' The singers, then ?'

I : ' Still less.'

E. : ' Well, then, it must be Reichardt's own music of which you disapprove ! Do not be afraid to say so.'

I : ' Excuse me ! The music, I repeat, is so

fine, that I could envy the composer, if envy were possible to a man of my way of thinking.'

E.: 'Then, you would shift the blame to the poet?'

I shrugged my shoulders.

E.: 'Well, well! I rather pique myself on my dramatic instincts, and hitherto I have failed to find a single fault in the piece. Perhaps you have keener sight. Please tell me if you have found one.'

I: 'I could wish that all the pieces I have set, and perhaps shall still have to set, were as pure as this.'

E.: 'You are getting a little beyond me. You praise the poem and the music; you make no objection to the singers and the orchestra; and yet you hesitate to prophesy a real success.'

I: 'Alas! I do. But please do not ask me to prove my point, until my prophecy has been fulfilled.'

I never can say enough about the kindness and attention which I met with from Herr Reichardt. He anticipated all my wishes with the greatest delicacy, and devoted much of his time to looking after me. When he called at my house, he gave me a list of some ten places where I had a standing invitation to dine or sup, so that I was forced to make entries in my pocket-book, for fear of forgetting my engagements. One evening, he took me to Madame Rietz, the King's friend, who subsequently became Countess Lichtenau.

She received me very politely, telling me that she had just been commissioned by the King to offer me a seat in her box, whenever there was anything going on at the opera. In the same way, she asked me to dine or sup with her, whenever I came to Charlottenburg.

Two days after, the King arrived, and Reichardt told me at once that His Majesty would speak to me next day at the concert. That same evening he came to fetch me, and drove me to Court in one of the Royal carriages. We had hardly entered the *salon*, when the King was told that we were there. He came up to me, was very gracious, and talked a great deal, telling me, amongst other things, that he had ordered a performance of my ' Doktor und Apotheker,' with other operas and plays, which were to be given in the theatre at Charlottenburg. Would I be so good as to undertake the task of conducting my own work?

When the whole Court came in, he addressed me in words of condescending kindness :

' Come, I want to introduce you to my sister, and to the Queen !

He did so, and Their Royal Highnesses were most gracious, and loaded me with civilities.

I had sent the King six new symphonies shortly before my arrival in Berlin ; one of them was given at the beginning, and another at the end of the concert. I appeared at every one of these concerts during my stay. This was a special distinction, for, as a rule, no one was invited who did not belong to the Court. Besides the King's own singers and *virtuosi*, I also heard Princess Friederike, his daughter by his first marriage (afterwards Duchess of York), as well as the Princess of Orange. They were both pianistes—better pianistes than one could have expected people of such high rank to be. The *virtuosi*—specially Duport the cellist, Ritter the bassoon-player, Balza and Thür-schmid, French-horn-players, and several others —did what one could only expect masters of these various instruments to do. Without going into details, I will merely say that they were quite worthy to be members of a Royal orchestra.

After ten or twelve tumultuous days in Berlin, I began to wonder whether I could give a performance of my oratorio ' Hiob,' for my own benefit, before the departure of the Hereditary Statthalterin. Reichardt not only approved of the idea, but was kind enough to advise me and lend a helping hand. Acting on his instructions, I posted a letter to the King, asking for his permission to employ the Court singers and orchestra, proposing at the same time that the performance should be given either in the garrison or the Castle church.

I got an answer next morning. The entire orchestra was placed at my disposal, but the King explained that he would be glad if I would substitute the National Theatre for the churches proposed.

That theatre, however, seemed to me hardly large enough for my purpose, so I ventured to write again, asking leave of the King to give my oratorio in the Grand Opera-house. He graciously answered that, although he had never before granted such a favour to anyone, and never intended to in the future, he was yet willing to make an exception in my favour. This led to a conference with Baron von der Reck, Directeur des Spectacles, who had already been instructed to assist me in every particular.

Whilst busy about the preparations, in which I was loyally assisted by Reichardt, I happened to hear two performances of the two grand Italian operas, ' Medea ' and ' Protesilao.' My readers will doubtless be anxious to know what I thought of them. I will give them my candid opinion, only mentioning by the way that both these operas had been given a year before, so there was nothing new about them.

The first was ' Medea,' which the Elector of Saxony's Kapellmeister, Herr Naumann, had set to music. It was worthy of a Naumann; he had spared neither art nor industry. He may have tried to be concise, but the opera lasted for six mortal hours—an unpardonable fault on the part of the poet, for he not only damages himself and condemns the public to endless *ennui*, but sacrifices even the best of composers at the same time. Who can possibly sit and listen to music for six hours on end, even if it come straight from Olympus?

Eager as I was, and full of rapt attention, my patience only held out for *four* hours, and the last two were sheer agony. I seemed to be sitting at the wedding-feast of a rich citizen, where, after tasting twenty dishes, one is asked to try another ten courses. Even amongst the singers and in the orchestra, I observed signs of weariness and slackness; they had been well together before, but now there was an uncertainty, which seemed to be the result, not of incapacity, but of disgust and repulsion.

Madame Todi and Signor Concialini, who took the chief parts, acted and sang admirably. The choruses, contrary to my expectation, were very well sung, and declaimed with a perfect Italian accent. Herr Lauchery, the ballet-master, had distinguished himself in the invention and arrangement of the dances. The solo-dancers, both men and women, were perfect in their art. I forget many of their names, and can only specify Demoiselle Redt-wein (now Madame Cloose) and Demoiselle Meroni, who were both first-rate. The scenery, by Herr Verona, was fully up to the mark of his great reputation, especially in the ballet where the sibyl allows Medea to look into the future. The entire ballet was represented behind a veil, drawn like a curtain before one of the *coulisses*, and the effect was very good, for you saw the dance as if through a thin mist. But there were some scenes so clumsily managed that they would not have passed muster in a theatre for marionettes—for example, the bulls breathing fire from their nostrils and ploughing the field. The dragon guarding the Golden Fleece was a wretched creature; Concialini, who acted Jason, was idiotic enough to strike the pasteboard tail of the wretched beast several times with the flat of his sword, making it ring

again.   It reminded me of the Bacchante *fête*
at Schlosshof, when the comic knights were
pummelled by the dummy satyrs.   I was so
disgusted that I forgot myself, and called out,
'*Pfui!*'

Madame Rietz looked round, and said :

'This is atrocious!   I shall tell him to-
morrow what I heard a great connoisseur say,
and I answer for it that he will change his
behaviour, for he is an intimate friend of mine,
and will be glad to take my advice.'

Now for the second opera, 'Protesilao!'   It
must be remembered that the first act is by
Reichardt, the second by Naumann.   Everyone in Berlin noticed this, and thought that
there was some rivalry.   However, the matter
stood thus.

When Naumann had given a performance
of his 'Medea' the year before, the King had
asked him whether he would protract his stay
in Berlin for another three months, during
which interval he might compose the music
for 'Protesilao,' which was to be performed in
honour of the reigning Queen's birthday.
Naumann told the King that he would very
gladly stay, but that so short an interval as
three months would hardly suffice for him to
write one half of the opera.

Was Naumann acting a part, or was he really a slow worker? Both questions are a puzzle to me. Speaking for myself, I could have fulfilled the King's wishes in two months, without trying my strength in any way. My experiences in the year 1786 prove this, for, from the beginning of January to the end of October in that year, I wrote five long works: 'Hiob,' 'Der Apotheker,' 'Betrug durch Aberglauben,' 'Democrito,' and 'Die Liebe im Narrenhause.' Now, had I wanted, as Naumann did, a term of six months for each of these works, instead of ten months for them all, I should have taken two years and a half over the business. But however that may be, the King let himself be talked over, and the two Kapellmeisters worked together in common as he wished. With a view to strict fairness, they cast lots for the choice of acts; the first fell to Reichardt, the second to Naumann. Naumann had not yet finished his act by the time Reichardt had finished both, and Reichardt gave him the second in a sealed envelope, which he was not to open till he had finished his own. A long while afterwards Naumann also wrote the first act, and his opera was given in Berlin, some years later. I cannot compare the two, for I know nothing about them.

I can say thus much about the libretto—that it is a pendant to Calsabiggi's 'Orfeo,' for which Gluck wrote music that is historical.

Before the opera began, Madame Rietz said to me:

'I am anxious to know whose music you think the best?'

'I had rather not answer that question,' I replied, 'for in such a case you are always obliged to praise one at the cost of the other.'

'But I must tell you,' said she, 'that the King has commissioned me to get your opinion, and I am sure you will be good enough to do him the favour.'

This was really putting the knife to my throat, but the opera lasted so long that I had time enough to plan a subterfuge.

'Now,' said Madame Rietz, when it was over, 'what do you think?'

I: 'Reichardt's music is full of life and fire; Naumann's, on the contrary, is restrained and temperate. Each composer has done his duty, each has written true music, and consequently it suits the text.'

Madame Rietz · 'All very well! but surely one must be in better taste than the other?'

I: 'I am not going to say that offhand, Madame. It would be premature even to say that Reichardt succeeds better in the fiery, and Naumann in the softer, passages, for it may only appear to be so.'

Madame Rietz: 'How so? Appear to be? Is it not a fact?'

I: 'No, Madame. Let us suppose that the lot had fallen out differently; who can say beforehand that both would not have worked with equal success?'

Madame Rietz: 'I admire your delicacy, but it will not satisfy the King.'

I: 'I am sorry for that, but I cannot help myself. Supposing each of the men had set the entire work, it might be criticised more justly; then I would have given my opinion without reserve, and spared no one. But as matters stand, you yourself must see that my judgment would be not only premature, but rash, and I should lay myself open to an imputation of unpardonable partiality.'

Madame Rietz (smiling): 'So far as I can see, you take very good care of yourself; you touch the prickles most daintily.'

Next day, Reichardt and I drove to Charlottenburg in one of the King's carriages. The Royal favourite had invited us to dinner and supper. Reichardt told me that I was the King's guest whenever I went there, and that

Madame Rietz was commissioned to do the honours of the household—a distinction but rarely accorded by the King to anyone.

I found her seated on a sofa, with a girl of some twelve years of age by her side ; a little boy of five, with whom she was playing, stood in front of her.

'That is my daughter by the King,' she said at once, 'the Gräfin von der Mark ; and this is my son by my own husband.'

Soon after this, two people of importance, great favourites with the King, appeared on the scene ; you can easily guess who one of them was ! The whole party strolled about for some time in the garden, and then adjourned to a table on the banks of the Spree, where covers were laid for nine persons. Eight servants, in Royal livery, were in attendance, and the whole service was of massive silver. The food and wine were, by command, the same as if the King himself had been present. An Italian opera buffa, 'Il Falegname,' was performed in the theatre at Charlottenburg, but in such wretched style, that I could not enough admire the patience with which the whole Court sat out three hours of such absurd music, so badly sung.

Supper was served afterwards, in the rooms

which the King liked best to occupy when he was alone at Charlottenburg. I was very much struck with the taste and elegance of everything that I saw; nothing could exceed the beauty of the decorations. It was past midnight when Reichardt and I drove off to Berlin, escorted by two Royal grooms carrying torches.

The day was approaching when 'Der Apotheker' was to be given at Charlottenburg. 'Hiob' was fixed for a later date. Four days before, I had to settle another dispute between Madame Baranius and Demoiselle Hellmuth, who both wanted the part of Rosalie. When one knows the importance attached to such matters by theatrical people, how every sort of passion and party spirit is aroused, and heaven and earth—or, what is much more to the purpose, theatres and coffee-houses—are all agog, the embarrassment resulting from this mighty question may be imagined. Engel sided with Hellmuth, who had taken the part during the indisposition of Baranius; but the latter insisted on her former right of possession, and, in addition to that, most of the other actors were on her side. I was chosen as arbiter, and voted, as may be supposed, for justice and beauty. My decision was applauded in the town, and I was called 'a charming man.'

At Madame Baranius' request, I went through her part with her, improving her singing, declamation and action; she was very easy to teach and very grateful. It was obvious, at the first rehearsal, that she acted with double the spirit, and the change induced Mademoiselle Unzelmann, who was an admirable actress, to ask a similar favour. Unquestionably, not the faintest hint of improvement was lost upon her. The new theatre built by the King was not yet ready, and the theatre in the Orangerie was but a small one; there was only room for an orchestra of thirty-six players. Monsieur Vachon, first violinist and leader of the King's band, was a friend of mine, so he chose a select number of the band, and my opera was beautifully executed. With the trifling exception of two cadence passages in the *ensemble* for the orchestra and singers, I was quite content with the performance, at the first rehearsal. When it was over, all the members of the orchestra asked if I were satisfied with them.

'Yes, gentlemen,' I said, 'if only you are satisfied with my conducting!'

Then Vachon spoke for the rest.

'*Voilà ce qu'on appelle diriger l'Orchestre, sans faire tant de bruit et des grimasses inutiles, qui ne servent qu'à barbouiller l'Orchestre!*'

Quite satisfied with that single rehearsal, I was going to stop the one fixed for next day, but the orchestra and the actors, though flattered by my explanation, asked for it themselves, in order to make things safe, and I gave way.

The same zealous spirit animated one and all at the performance, which went so well that I had not a wish unsatisfied. Between the first and second acts, the King came up to the orchestra, and said to me :

'You have altered your opera, and very much improved it.'

'Not a note has been changed,' I replied.

'Impossible!' said the King.

'Upon my honour !'

'I have heard the opera eight times,' he continued, 'but to-day the music sounds so graceful, so new ! How is that ?'

'I owe it to Your Majesty's incomparable orchestra.'

'And I to your conducting,' replied the King.

Turning to Vachon, he said :

'*Monsieur de Dittersdorf est très content de vous.*'

'*Ah, sire !*' answered Vachon '*Sous sa Direction nous sommes prêts de le suivre au milieu de l'enfer.*'

I must not omit a slight incident, which occurred during the performance of my piece.

The theatre, as I said before, was built in the great Orangerie, and the gardener's lodge adjoining it was converted into dressing-rooms for the actors. Guards were stationed at each door, and also at that by which the actors reached the stage, so as to prevent officious intrusion. Before the opera began, they were passed through the ranks of the Guards by the inspector, the Guards having been strictly ordered to admit none but the actors and persons who had to do with the theatre. Lippert, who, as Surgeon Sichel, had to assume a woman's dress in the second act, passed through as a man, and again claimed admission, as a woman.

'Get back there, you bad woman!' shouted the sentinel, and threatened to punch him in the ribs with the butt end of his musket. 'Go to the deuce with you! We do not want such *canaille* here. *Allons*, march!'

Fortunately, the Inspector of Theatres heard the altercation and intervened. The blundering Moravian looked like a fool, and stroked his moustache, muttering to himself, 'What a stupid blockhead I am! Who would have thought of it? Why, the fellow looks as if he had just escaped from the Penitentiary!'

Well, I must get my 'Hiob' performed at last! But it was not so easy. I had made arrangements with all my singers; the only one to throw up her part was Madame Todi. She excused herself, on the ground that her chest had suffered so much from rehearsals and the four performances of '*quell' opere eterne*,' as she justly called those never-ending works, that she could not sing in my oratorio with all the energy which the music required. Demoiselle Niclas, formerly first singer of the Margraf von Schwedt, cheerfully undertook the part, and sang it admirably.

Herr Gasparini, the Inspector of the Grand Opera-house, had cleared the stage, now that no more operas were to be given there, and had set up the fine scenery of the Redoutensaal. I ordered in the scenic decorations out of 'Protesilao,' which gave me a splendid gallery in the middle of the stage, and several staircases, steps, and balustrades, which formed a very agreeable *coup d'œil*. The gallery was white, with gold tracery, which harmonized admirably with the Redoutensaal; it was so roomy, too, that there was ample space for more than three hundred people. I posted about eighty persons *à plein pied;* the other members of the orchestra were distributed in groups, tier upon tier in the gallery, so symmetrically that the *ensemble* was quite a feast for the eyes of the audience. The effect was enhanced by the splendid light thrown from fifty chandeliers on the desks of some hundred players. Some of these carried twenty-four, others twelve or eighteen lights. Between every box in the amphitheatre there was a wall-chandelier with two lights. The effect was magnificent, but it was at the cost of ninety-four pounds of wax candles.

Honest Reichardt undertook the management of the chorus, which consisted of eighty persons, and of all the musicians who were not members of the Royal band ; he acquitted himself so well that my oratorio was rendered by an orchestra consisting of some *two hundred and thirty persons.*

With two rehearsals I had everything in perfect order, but what a shock I experienced on the day before the performance, when I calculated the full cost ! Although I had the services of the entire Royal orchestra for nothing, as well as those of a great number of amateurs, I had still to pay half the band and the chorus.

Everybody got one thaler for a rehearsal, and two for a performance.   Here is my bill :

Orchestra	480 Reichsthaler.
Copyists ...	230 ,,
Wax candles	80
Posters, box-keeper, gratuities, advertisements in the newspapers, item *affiches*	70
Total	860 Reichsthaler.

—which, in Imperial money, represented a sum of twelve hundred and ninety florins.

When I had made this out, conceive what I suffered from anxiety, for it was still quite uncertain whether I should have a large or a small audience ! I had abandoned all hope of any profits; I was afraid that I might lose heavily ; but Providence favoured me.   In spite of the enormous expenses, I realized a considerable sum.

After deducting my travelling expenses to and fro, besides maintenance in Berlin, which amounted in all to seven hundred and eighty-five florins, I had a clear overplus of two thousand six hundred and seventy-five gulden. Consequently, I had taken four thousand seven hundred and fifty florins in the Opera-house.

This, I dare say, will seem to many incredible, for, if my calculation is correct, the amphitheatre in the Berlin Opera-house must be at least five times larger than that of the Kärnthnerthor at Vienna, which, when crowded to the roof, never realizes more than eight hundred and twenty florins ; and it must be remembered that the Kärnthnerthor has five extra *étages*, whereas there are only three at Berlin. But the matter is explained when I add that, in lieu of the fixed price for tickets of admission, I often received two, three, four, six, even eight Friedrichs d'or. The Princess of Orange asked for four tickets, and paid me forty Friedrichs d'or for them.

Talking of tickets, a very unusual thing occurred. On the morning of the performance, people were coming in crowds to get them, and amongst others a common soldier turned up, who asked me, in the lowest Moravian dialect, to give him one, at the same time throwing down on the table a little paper packet.

'Here are twenty-four four-groschen pieces, four thalers,' said he, as he pounced on the ticket and was about to decamp.

'Stop, my friend!' cried I. 'It is a mistake —the ticket only costs two thalers.'

But he was off in a moment. When I opened the packet, lo and behold, twenty-four Friedrichs d'or! I never could find out who it was that sent the money. But think of the soldier's honesty! for the packet was not sealed, and no one ever asked me whether I had received the sum or not.

It does not become me to do more than hint at the success of my oratorio, and the generosity and kindness shown to me by the critics of Berlin. The public journals praised every note of it, and the performance was signalized as a great artistic festival, which it really was.

Next day, I was dining with a dear old Viennese friend, Colonel Fabian, when I was called out to receive a messenger with a heavy packet and a letter from Rietz, the Controller of the Privy Purse, in which he said that the King had commissioned him to give me the enclosed, as a souvenir of yesterday's perform ance. It was a large gold snuff-box, enamelled in blue, and containing two hundred ducats. I was really touched by the distinction conferred on me by this good King, who venerated art, and delighted in showing delicate attentions to those whose profession it was. On the very last day of my stay in Berlin, I was his guest at dinner and supper at Charlottenburg, and my kind hostess exceeded, if possible, her former efforts to give me pleasure, and to make me feel happily conscious that I was a special favourite with her Royal protector.   I was about to go, when she said :

'Should you ever want anything from the King, and I can be of any service, be sure you apply to me!   I shall always be delighted to advance your interests as best I may.'

Reichardt and I started for Berlin soon after midnight.   By half-past one, my son and I were seated in our carriage.   We travelled day and night till we reached Breslau, arriving there on the fourth day.   I had previously made all the arrangements necessary for the performance of my 'Hiob.'   The orchestra consisted of one hundred persons, and, after all expenses paid, I realized a little over two hundred thalers.   Rich in honour and in money, I returned to Johannisberg, and met the smiling faces of my family, and the friendly but inquiring glance of my creditors.

CHAPTER XXVII.

Illness of the *Prince*-Bishop—My conversation with him.

JOHANNISBERG had lost much of its former
brightness. The Prince-Bishop of Breslau was
becoming more and more despondent. It was
trying to him to live, as it were, the life of a
pensioner, in a place where he was once in a
position of command, and where he was forced
to look on, whilst others were docking the
salaries of his officials, and appointing foreigners
in their stead, even among the huntsmen, without consulting him. He had tried repeatedly
to induce the Emperor, Joseph II., to get rid
of the Administration, and enable him once
again to manage his own property, but in vain.
Joseph died, and then the Prince turned to the
Emperor Leopold, who quite unexpectedly reinstated him. The good news was forwarded
to him, through his agent, by a special
messenger from Vienna, who arrived early in

the morning, and that very same day he gave a large dinner-party, and restored his former dependents to active service, at their former salary.

But the old trouble had completely undermined his health, and a few months after the change he had a serious illness, which finally culminated in putrid fever. Stolle, his body-physician, though convinced of the possibility of saving his life, agreed to call in several other doctors, in accordance with our wishes, and a *consilium medicum* was held. All six of them, Stolle excepted, pronounced the case to be hopeless ; he adhered to his opinion, and the event proved that he was right The medicines unanimously prescribed by his six colleagues only made the patient weaker. Stolle summoned us old servants, and warned us that the Prince would die under the present *régime ;* he vouched for his recovery, if we would consent that the patient should adopt his treatment. We did consent ; the good Prince's improvement was obvious three days afterwards, and on the sixth day he was completely out of danger. The one bad symptom left was a weakness in the feet, which prevented him from taking exercise without the help of two men. Stolle's skill added nearly five years to his life.

'It pains me to think,' said the worthy doctor, 'that, for the few sad years remaining, the mind will gradually be so affected that the Prince will never be able to manage his own affairs nor those of his diocese. He will lose all zest for amusements—music, for instance; he may become childish; I fear, too, he may be misled into doing foolish acts, under the influence of certain people who are about him. There is but little danger, so long as you, the Landeshauptmann, and President von Gambsberg, your brother-in-law, are near him; but the steward is consumptive, and has not three months to live, and Gambsberg has too much to do. Your support, therefore, is all that I have to rely upon.'

There never lived a more truthful prophet than the worthy Stolle. The Landeshaupt mann died before the three months were out, and though the Prince had promised that I should be allowed to exchange my office at Freyenwaldau for the more lucrative post at Johannisberg, I was jockeyed out of the appointment by an odious intriguer, who induced the Prince to give it to him.

The dead man was not yet buried, when I noticed a sudden coldness and indifference towards myself on the part of the Prince, who, for many years, had honoured me with the strictest confidence. It was obvious not only to myself, but to every well-disposed person, that I had been crowded out, only that others might get at the weak side of the good gentleman, and make hay while the sun shone. Herr von Gambsberg and I represented this to the Prince, but a sworn conspiracy was already on foot, and an answer had been put into his mouth. It was to the effect that we should not venture to give advice unless called for, nor to appear unless we were summoned.

The leading principle of this conspiracy was, not only to withhold from the Prince and to render distasteful everything calculated to cheer him, but to keep the good man in perpetual terror of death, so as to divert his attention from the mean doings of the conspirators. They persuaded him that he was in hourly danger of dying of apoplexy, and he became so despondent that he actually began to be childish.

This unlucky business brought on me an attack of gout, though, by the help of Stolle, I was able to get about again with crutches in a fortnight's time. Stolle came daily, and told me of all the mischief that was brewing,

' Do go yourself to the Castle,' he said to me

one day, 'and see the Prince! He always trusted you. Tell him the truth as plainly as you can ; that may perhaps rouse him.'

'But what if I get a rebuff?'

'Well, then you can try again!'

I determined to follow his advice.

Long experience had taught me that, if you wanted to make the Prince take notice, you must attract his attention by something unusual.

Cards had been substituted for music in the evenings by his companions ; they used to play commerce at two or more tables, and the Prince was brought in, in an armchair, to watch the game.

I hobbled up to him, leaning on my stick. Everybody stared and started—particularly one fine gentleman playing taroc at a small table. The Prince and I conversed as follows ·

Prince: 'What do you want ? I did not summon you.'

I (in a stern, determined tone) · 'So much the worse, Your Highness, that you should treat me so ungraciously, at the very moment when I am most wanted!' (To a servant, standing behind the Prince's chair :) 'Hulloa, you clown ! what are you gaping there for ? Do you not see that I cannot bear to stand

Bring me a chair!' (The servant fetches one.) 'Put it here, close to the Prince!'

I sat down.

Prince : 'You are damnably familiar.'

I : 'If a man like that gentleman there is allowed to sit down, I have ten times the right.'

Prince : 'You are determined, I see, to be impudent.'

I · 'Heaven forbid! How could I be ? But they told me that Your Highness was failing, and I thought, " My master may die without being reconciled to me," so I made up my mind to crawl here as soon as I could, that I might tell Your Highness that I forgive you everything, and you are not to suffer on my account in the next world.'

Prince (deeply moved and embarrassed) : 'What ? How ? You forgive me ? What have I done to you ?'

I (coldly) : 'I did not come here to reproach Your Highness, but' (looking the Prince full in the face) 'I see now that the dying will take some years yet!' (To the servant :) 'Bring those candles from the table! Look at me, Your Royal Highness !' (After a pause :) 'The eyes are fresh; plenty of colour in the face; respiration good. How is the appetite, if I may ask ?'

Prince : 'Well—I can eat !'

I : ' And sleep ?'

Prince : ' I sleep tolerably.'

I : ' Well, in the name of wonder, then, what is all this talk about danger ?'

Prince : 'Why, apoplexy comes on just at the moment when one least expects it !'

I : ' Your Royal Highness is as far from apoplexy as I am from Nova Zembla.'

Prince : ' How can you say that ?'

I : ' Experience teaches me Prince Hildburghausen has suffered from the same disease for the last nineteen years. He can neither walk nor stand, yet he still lives, and in his eighty-eighth year he is as fresh and bright as ever.'

Prince (with a sigh) : ' That will never be my fate.'

I : ' Why not ?'

Prince : ' Do you think it will ?'

I : ' Certainly I do,—if Your Royal Highness starts upon another course of life. As you are living now, every door and window is open to death, whereas you ought to bolt and bar everything, to keep death away.'

Prince · ' How can I do that ?'

I : ' By putting a bright face upon everything. Forgive me for saying so, but Your Highness

is afraid where no fear is.   That is unmanly—
I might say childish—and Your Highness is so
good and so wise!   Only thick-blooded people
need dread apoplexy; you have thin blood,
which will turn thick, if you sit there like a
brood-hen, hatching one fad after another.   It
is that which makes thick blood.   Be cheerful;
that will make it thin.'

Prince: 'How can I be cheerful?'

I: 'Your Royal Highness can best answer
that question for yourself.'

Prince: 'But I want your opinion.'

I: 'Well, Your Highness had better do the
very opposite of everything you are doing now.'

Prince · 'How?'

I: 'First of all, you must give up—for a
time, at all events—your duties as a Bishop
and a Prince.   Herr von Gambsberg can look
after the one, your worthy spiritual counsellors
the other.   In the second place, entrust the
superintendence of your household, which has
been an endless source of trouble to you, to
some honest man.'

Prince · 'You would be the very one.'

I: 'I have found another little place for
myself.'

Prince: 'And that is?'

I: 'I will be your Mentor, out of pure love,

assuming that you promise me not to reward
my good advice with coldness and disdain, as
you have done.'

Prince: 'But you would have to be with
me continually.'

I: 'With all my heart!'

Prince · 'Why, then you could undertake
the household as well.'

I: 'So be it, on the express understanding
that I have *plein pouvoir.*'

Prince: 'That you shall have.'

I: 'Thirdly, you must render blind obedience
to your good physician Stolle, who saved your
life once, and will preserve it for a long time
yet.'

Prince: 'With all my heart!'

I: 'There is a good deal yet to be said
about all sorts of things that may amuse and
cheer you. I have many a design *in petto*, of
which Your Highness is sure to approve.'

I knew the Prince well enough to foresee
that my *in petto* would tickle his curiosity; so
long as I kept the secret from him, I felt certain
that he would not let himself be distracted. So
I got up and said :

'I am a convalescent, and am obliged to
spare myself. If Your Royal Highness
pleases——'

Prince: ' Oh, please stay ! You are like the Good Samaritan, pouring balsam into my wounds.'

I (after resuming my seat) : ' Why have we no music to-day ?'

Prince : ' There has been none for several days past.'

I : ' That is wrong. Why are we to have none ?'

Prince : ' Alas ! it only makes me more wretched.'

I (smiling) : ' I do not think it would. It would have the very opposite effect upon your spirits.'

Prince: ' Do you think so ? I will follow your advice ! Let us have music again every evening ; we will begin to-morrow.'

I : ' Thank Heaven for that ! All will be well now.'

I began to say good-bye.

Prince: ' When are you coming back again ?'

I : ' If to-morrow be as fine as to-day, expect me for the concert, and I will bring a new symphony with me.'

I kissed the Prince's hand, and he dismissed me very graciously.

FAREWELL.

THUS, I had voluntarily undertaken the burdensome duty of being in constant attendance upon the Prince. Every evening, when I followed him to his bedroom after supper, I had to promise that I would return to the Castle at eight o'clock next morning. Such was my duty, day by day.

I soon observed that most of the servants, now long accustomed to idleness, were very awkward when they had to lead or carry the Prince, who could not go a step alone, and I showed them how they could make matters less troublesome to him and to themselves as well. With all his retinue of servants, I thought that the Prince was badly served. Many a time the antechamber was crowded with these good-for-nothing fellows, and just when they were particularly wanted, not a man was within call. I often preached to them, but it did no good ; so at last I summoned the whole lot, and told them that, as they would not listen to kind words, I should try harsh measures.

' Two of you must be in attendance on the Prince, turn and turn about, every day for twenty-four hours, and you will have to sleep in the antechamber. As there are eight of you, each will take his turn every fifth day ; but the others must serve personally at their master's table. If anyone shirks, I shall deduct a gulden from his pay, and put it into the poor-box.'

I carried this out in the case of two rascally *valets-de-chambre*, for I found piles of dust, not only in the Prince's bedroom, but also an inch thick on the stove in the sitting-room, not to mention other disagreeables.

Once more good order prevailed at the Castle, and the Prince was quite delighted. With such a mob at my heels, I had many enemies, but I did not trouble myself about these.

We had such rough, stormy weather one evening when I was there, that the Prince told me I had better stay at the Castle, and he would order a bedroom for me near his own. Accordingly, I stayed. The Prince retired to bed ; I sat near him in an armchair, and talked to him until he went off to sleep. He awoke, as his habit was, about three a.m., turned in bed, and remained awake for half an hour ; then he slept again until eight. Hearing from my bedroom, which adjoined his, that the Prince was restless, I put on my dressing-gown, and, sitting down at his bedside, stayed with him until he went to sleep again. He was so much pleased with this, that he often persuaded me to stop for the night, and at last it became a habit. In short, good - natured simpleton that I was, I remained at the Castle for two years and one month straight on end, leading such an uncomfortable life, that my present weakly state is largely attributable to it—all the more that it not only undermined my health in my fifty-fourth year, but left me in the state in which I now am : poor, and an invalid.

Six months had hardly passed before I grew very weary of the everlasting confinement, the want of exercise, and the very disturbed nights. But, having once determined to go through with it, I stuck to my resolution as long as I possibly could. After two years and a month, I was attacked by the most fearful hemorrhoidal pains, and I was obliged to shift from the Castle to my own house, on account of my health.

20

This was a golden opportunity for my enemies. During my absence, that notorious N., by dint of bribing one of the Prince's body-servants, and some lackeys of whom he was rather fond, contrived to get them over to his side, and to prejudice my case. I could give the names of all these rascals, but prefer to refuse them the honour of a record in the pages of a biography, in which I have introduced so many great and honoured persons.

A mine was sprung on me by these villainous plotters, and the Prince's suspicions were aroused, so that on April 7, 1794, I received an order never to enter the Castle again. I was to pack up my traps within a week, and be off to my official duties at Freyenwaldau. I should like to show my readers the miserable artifice by which my enemies made the Prince mistrust my loyalty, but he is in the grave, and the story might grievously hurt his good name, so let me draw a veil over it! I cannot, however, refrain from saying that I have proved my innocence, even at the Imperial Court. One of its high decrees completely acquitted me of dishonest behaviour, and besides that, I received proper compensation. I treasure the document as if it were gold, and can show it in its original form to anyone who may wish to see it. Can you wonder that my many injuries and *pathemata animi* brought me to a sick-bed in the end?

I fell ill at the end of October, 1794, and that was the beginning of my misery. Since then, I have not had one hour's good health. The doctors did all they could to bring on another attack of gout, so that the illness might run its usual course, but so far—and it is now five years since they began—they have not been successful.

The Prince died on January 5, 1795. An Imperial Administration succeeded, and it aimed at separating the property on-this-side from the bishopric of Breslau; but the King of Prussia took the bishopric under his protection. Both Courts negotiated for a considerable time, and at last it was agreed that the Administration should be abolished, and the property revert, as formerly, to the bishopric.

Prince Joseph of Hohenlohe-Bartenstein had already become Coadjutor before the death of the lamented Bishop, after which event he was made Bishop of Breslau. As usual, he had his own favourites to provide for, so I, my brother-in-law, and some other old officials, were pensioned off to make way for them.

Although I could show a record of twenty-six years of service, my annual pension came to no more than three hundred and thirty-three thalers eight groschen. My brother-in-law, von Gambsberg, who had served the bishopric for over forty years, got no more than I did. Before six months were out, the good man died, and his widow, my sister, now gets a miserable pittance of one hundred and thirty-three thalers eight groschen.

Since this epoch, a very sad one for me and my poor family, I have become so much worse that I am a regular cripple, and I have to be carried from my bed to the armchair, from my armchair to the bed. My resources, owing to the expenses of doctors, physic, and three sets of baths—those of Ullersdorf, Landeck, and Teschen—have dwindled to the last farthing, and last year, when a leading doctor of Baden, near Vienna, advised me to take the waters there, I found that I must despair of this remedy, for want of means. I long for my release.

Ignaz, Freiherr von Stillfried, happened to hear of my great poverty through a third person, and, quite unexpectedly, I received a consoling letter from him. It ran thus ·

' I have heard of your sad state. I have three houses on my property in Bohemia. Come to my arms, you and your family ! Neither you nor they shall starve. Let us pass the remainder of our days together !'

I joyfully accepted this kind offer, and I and my family, consisting of my wife, two sons and a daughter, five of us in all, threw ourselves on my dear friend's protection. Had I not chanced to find this benefactor, God knows, I should have perished long ago from poverty and misery; and after that—my dear ones? Oh God, let anyone who knows what that is measure the depth of it!

For nearly two years, I have been living on Baron Stillfried's property, Rothlhotta, in the Taborer district, near Neuhaus, free of cost, and yet I am still, in every respect, a beggar, for I have to pay every year in cash out of my pension:

Interest on mortgage debts	81 fl.
War-tax	60 „
House and ground rent ...	9 „
A servant, to help my son in lifting me and carrying me about; he has to watch, rather than to sleep, with me all night	120 „
A maidservant	36 „
Laundress...	45 „
Total	351 fl.

thus leaving me a surplus of one hundred and forty-nine florins. You may judge if such a sum enables me to clothe *five* people, and to pay other little necessary expenses.

My things disappear one after the other, to the tune of one-third or even less than one-third, I suppose, of their intrinsic value ; and when they are all gone, what then ?   For the last five years I have tasked my mental powers, which, Heaven be thanked ! are still tolerably good, in the production of many new works, such as operas, symphonies, and a great number of pianoforte compositions.   All these things were announced more than three months ago in the *Neue Musikalische Leipziger Zeitung*, but, good heavens ! not a soul has bought one single piece as yet ; and though I really give good money's worth, alas ! I cannot find a maintenance in that way.

I honour my dear good German nation, but when it comes to the question of maintenance, then, alas ! she is not at home.   Conscious as I am that my name and my works are known throughout all Europe, I may assume that I have given pleasure to half a million of people in this inhabited portion of the world.   If each unit were to throw me down *a single groschen in omni et toto*—or, still better, my family, for money is of no more use to me—how light would be the tax on the giver, and what a real support it would be for the desolate, neglected relatives of one who has not buried his talent in a napkin, like the man in the Gospel.

Dear reader, please do not suspect me of writing down what I have said above, in order to extract an alms from you for myself! Most likely I shall be no more, by the time you get this little book. When my tumbledown cottage has quite fallen into ruins, should anyone come to the rescue of my poor family, may the good Lord reward him!

I frankly own that I have brought my people into deep distress. Poverty in the first instance, and then my illness, was the cause. But my poverty should plead for me to some extent. I am not to blame for getting so small a pension after twenty-six years' service, nor for having to expend the last farthing that I had saved on doctors' bills, apothecaries' drugs, and baths, without deriving any benefit from them. Still, I am to blame for paying so little heed to my health,—all the more because kindly Nature endowed me with a firm and strong constitution, against which—fool that I was—I designedly made war. Alas! alas! I must exclaim with Father Horace:

'Quæ mens est hodie, cur eadem non puero fuit?
Vel cur bis animis incolumes non redeunt genæ?'

INDEX.

THE END.

BILLING AND SONS, PRINTERS, GUILDFORD.
G., C. & Co.

CPSIA information can be obtained
at www.ICGtesting.com
Printed in the USA
FSOW04n2015180416
19402FS

9 781330 311219